Some Architects' Portraits in Nineteenth-Century America

Personifying the Evolving Profession

Some Architects' Portraits in Nineteenth-Century America

Personifying the Evolving Profession

James F. O'Gorman

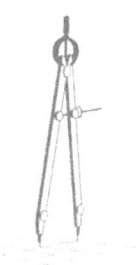

American Philosophical Society
Philadelphia • 2013

Transactions of the
American Philosophical Society
Held at Philadelphia
For Promoting Useful Knowledge
Volume 103, Part 4

ISBN: 978-1-60618-034-1

US ISSN:0065-97467

Library of Congress Cataloguing-in-Publication Data

O'Gorman, James F.
    Some architects' portraits in nineteenth-century America : personifying the evolving profession / James F. O'Gorman.
        pages cm. — (Transactions of the American philosophical society held at Philadelphia for promoting useful knowledge ; volume 103, part 4)
    Includes bibliographical references and index.
    ISBN 978-1-60618-034-1
    1. Portraits, American—19th century. 2. Architects—United States—Portraits. 3. Art and society—United States—History—19th century. I. Title.
N7593.2.O39 2013
740'.44092273—dc23
                        2013046155

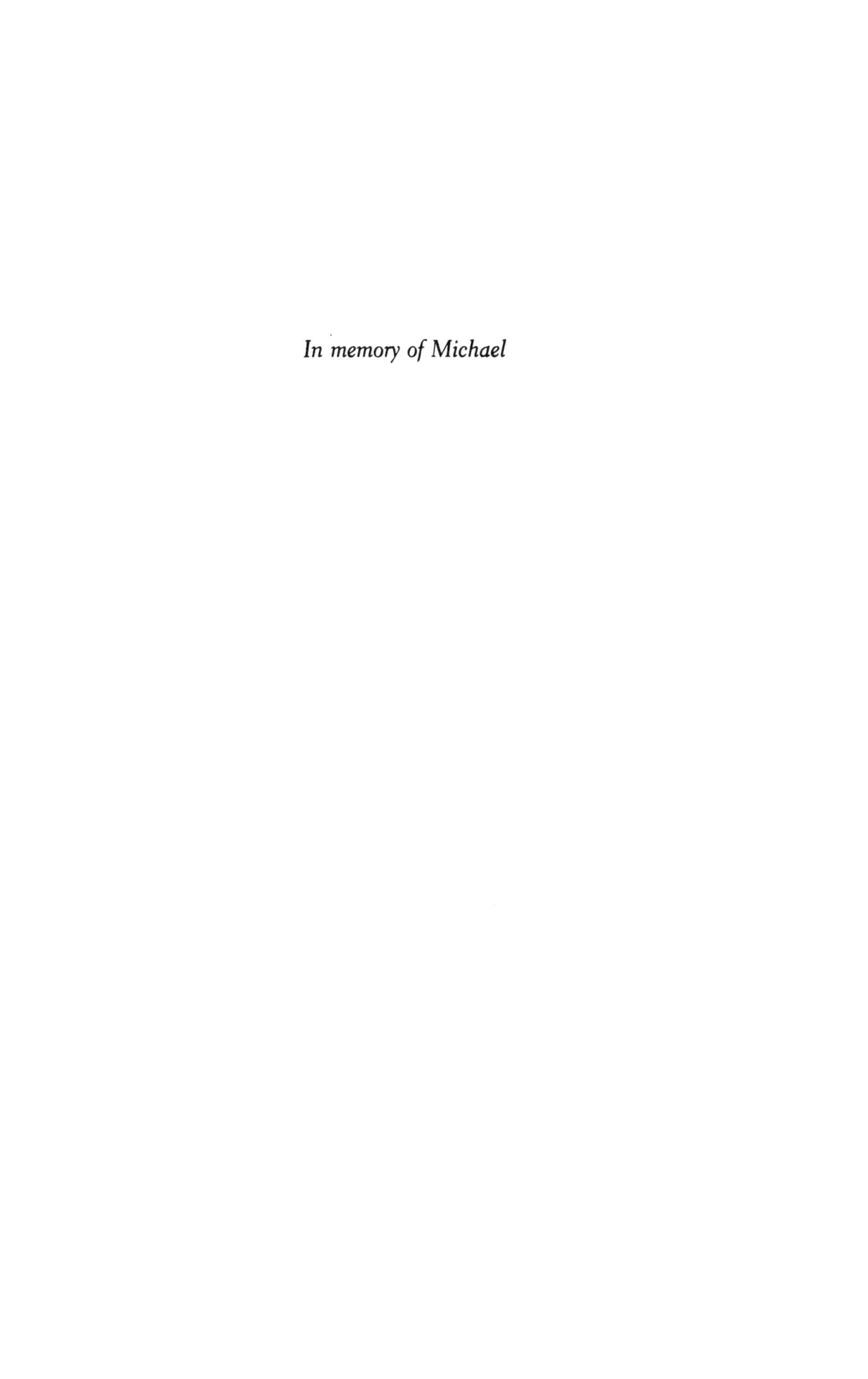

In memory of Michael

Contents

Preface

Of the two basic functions of portraiture, to limn an individual likeness or identify a type within the social fabric, this study is concerned with type.[1] Records of the individual likenesses of architects, head or head-and-shoulder images, including sculpted busts, occur in Western art into the present, and nineteenth-century America is no exception. Although they probably form a majority of portraits, such works are not the primary subject of this inquiry. From, say, Rembrandt Peale's of Baltimore's Maximilian Godefroy (1765–1840?) of about 1815, now on extended loan to the Maryland Historical Society, to John Singer Sargent's 1917 charcoal drawing of Boston's Guy Lowell (1870–1927) at that city's Museum of Fine Arts, an individual's physiognomy, and perhaps psychology, are the foci of such works, as they are with like portraits of anyone else. This, rather, is a selective overview of the iconography of a particular type, not of individual likeness or artistic quality, so Charles Willson Peale's head of Benjamin Henry Latrobe of 1804, for example, as fine a painting as it is, has no place here (although, as we shall see, other portraits of the architect do), whereas Elsa Koenig's early twentieth-century portrait of Philadelphia's Thomas Richards, a much lesser artistic achievement, does.[2] We shall pay special attention in this brief discussion to what besides the figure of the sitter appears in an architect's portrait. We shall also look at what the coeval state of the profession can tell us about such a drawn, painted, or photographed likeness, and, in contrast, what that image can tell us about the concurrent state of the profession.

NOTES

1. See Shearer West, *Portraiture* (New York: Oxford University Press, 2004).
2. In searching for appropriate portraits one must go as always to the original, but especially here, for in reproduction the image may be cropped to head or head and shoulders, leaving out all the visual information the iconographer needs. See note 41, chapter 2, for an example of cropping.

Acknowledgments

Financial support for this study came from the Helen S. French Fund for Faculty Awards at Wellesley College and a Franklin Research Grant from the American Philosophical Society. Among those whose help was indispensible are Andrew Alpern, Lilian Armstrong, Margherita Azzi-Visentini, Mary Beth Betts, Jeffrey Cohen, Lorna Condon, Mary Daniels, Peter Fergusson, Walter Gibson, Erica Hirshler, Rena M. Hoisington, Michael J. Lewis, Bonnie MacAdam, Sandra Olsen, Janet Parks, Peter Preston-Morley, Michael Ryan, Earle G. Shettleworth, Jr., Sandra Tatman, Wendy Watson, and the generous staffs of many museums, historical societies, and libraries.

Some Architects' Portraits in Nineteenth-Century America

Personifying the Evolving Profession

1

Prologue: Before 1800

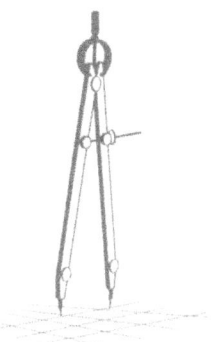

EUROPE

In 1772, Thomas-Germain-Joseph Duvivier of France depicted what is now the lost world of the architect in a painting housed at present in the Norton Simon Museum in Pasadena, California. *Le table de l'architecte* contains items, clearly used, that we associate with the work of the precomputer-aided designer of buildings and other structures, especially hand-crafted drawings and draftsman's needs, such as straightedge, ink, pens, reference books, and a pair of compasses placed front and center (Figure 1.1).[1] Duvivier was a pupil of Jean Baptiste Siméon Chardin, whose *Les attributs de l'architecte* of about 1725–30, now in the Art Museum at Princeton University, also shows drawings, books, a case of drafting instruments, rule, protractor, and a pair of dividers in the lower left corner.[2] Although the young architect of today would probably not recognize such obsolete tools, these instruments, as these paintings attest, once commonly functioned as extensions of the architect's hand in the drafting rooms of the Western world.[3] Among the implements shown, pairs of compasses or dividers, less often a scale, a porte-crayon, or a ruler traditionally identified the sitter as an architect, although not always, as we shall see.[4]

Now we often think of the T-square as the emblem of the past drafts-man-designer, but, although used much earlier,[5] the T-square did not become commonly associated with the architect until the latter part of the nineteenth century. Previous images of European or British architects most often include one or more drafting tools to signify the sitter's profession. A visual survey of the hundreds of prints created from painted portraits of Western architects found in such important collections as those at the Canadian Centre for Architecture in Montreal or in the Lawrence Hall Fowler Collection of portrait prints of architects at the Baltimore Museum of Art, demonstrates that a pair of dividers, often held by the sitter, at times shown idle on the drafting table, most frequently appear as emblems of the architect's profession. From portraits such as that by Nicolaes van Helt Stockade of the seventeenth-century Dutchman Simon Bosboom, architect, mason, and author of a work on the five orders taken from Vicenzo Scamozzi's treatise, who seems about to impale himself with his pair of dividers (Figure 1.2); through Henry Hornbostel's use of a quick-setting compass with legs spread to form the letter A for "Architecture" on the exterior of his College of Fine Arts at Carnegie Mellon University in Pittsburgh (1912–13); to Spiro Kostof's *The Architect,*

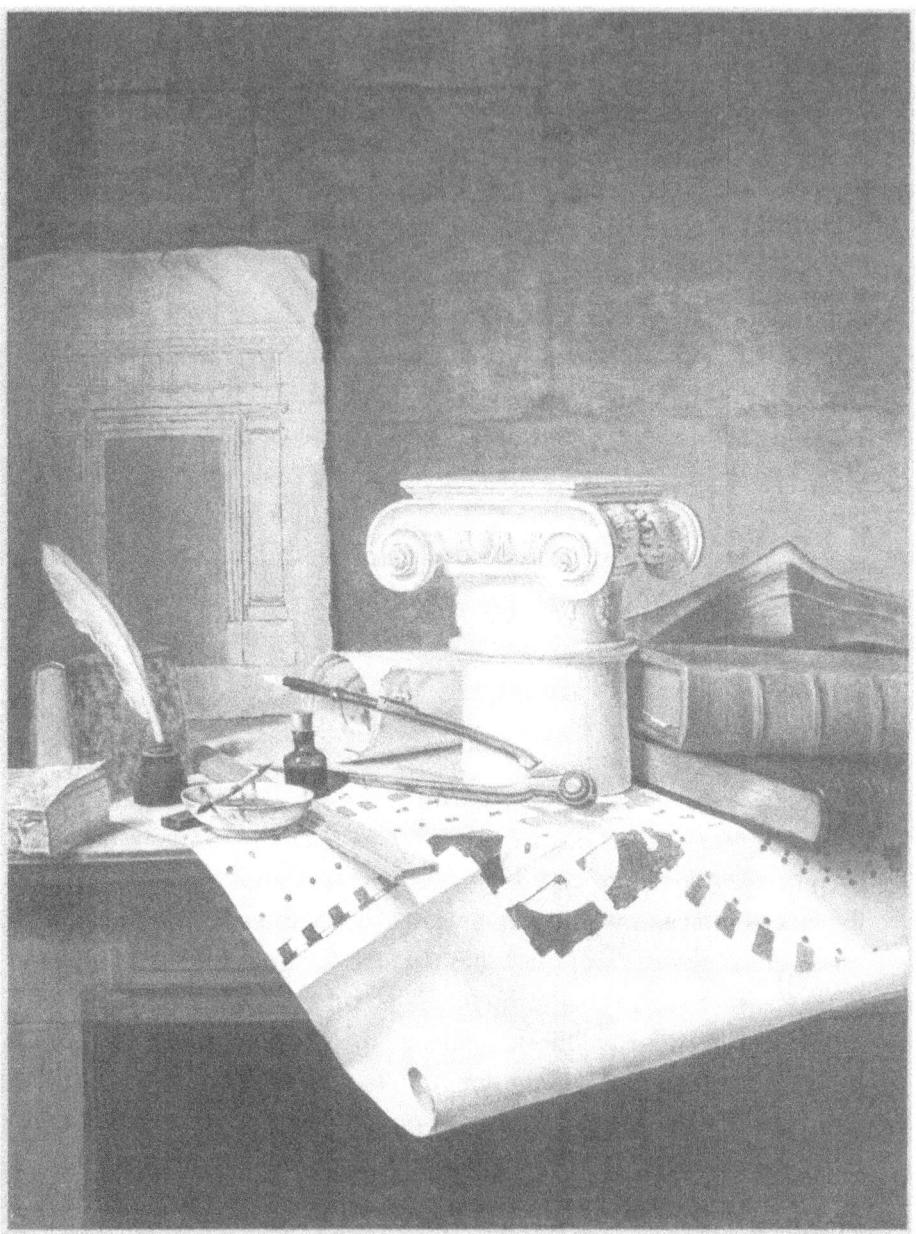

Figure 1.1   Thomas-Germain-Joseph Duvivier, *Le table de l'architecte*, 1772.
Reproduced courtesy of the Norton Simon Museum, Pasadena, California.

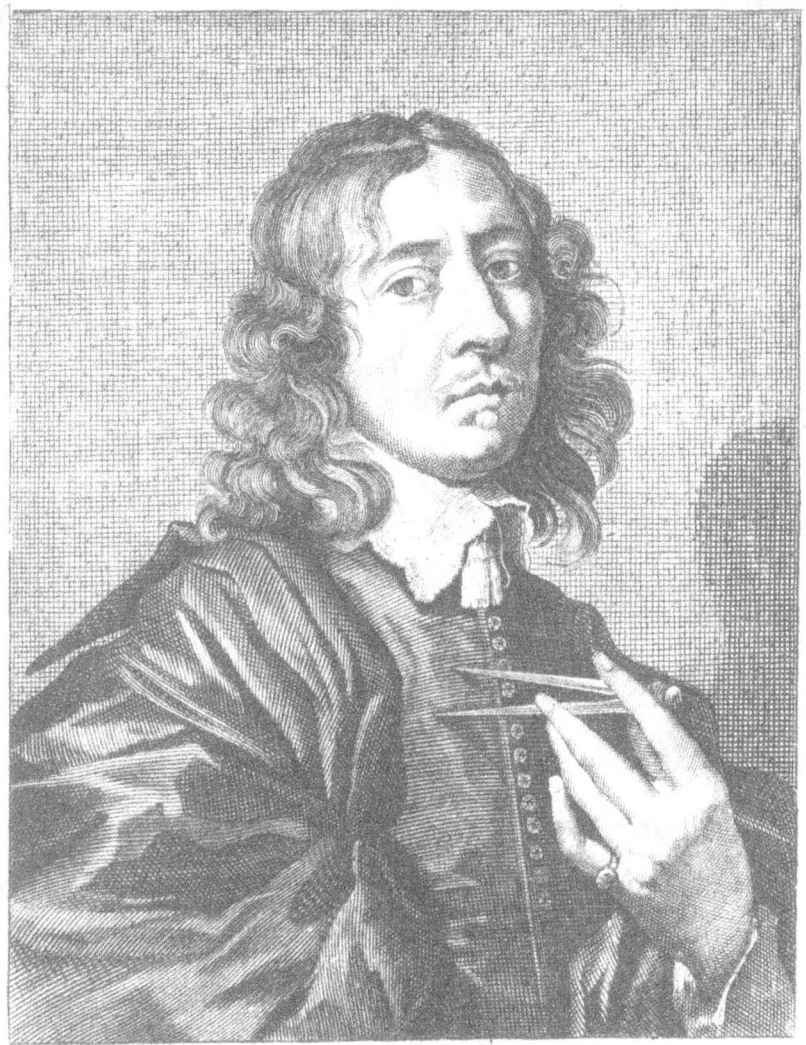

Figure 1.2   Pieter de Jode II after Nicolaes van Helt Stockade, engraving, *Simon Bos-boom*, 1662.

Reproduced courtesy of the Collection Centre Canadien d'Architecture/Canadian Centre for Architecture, Montreal.

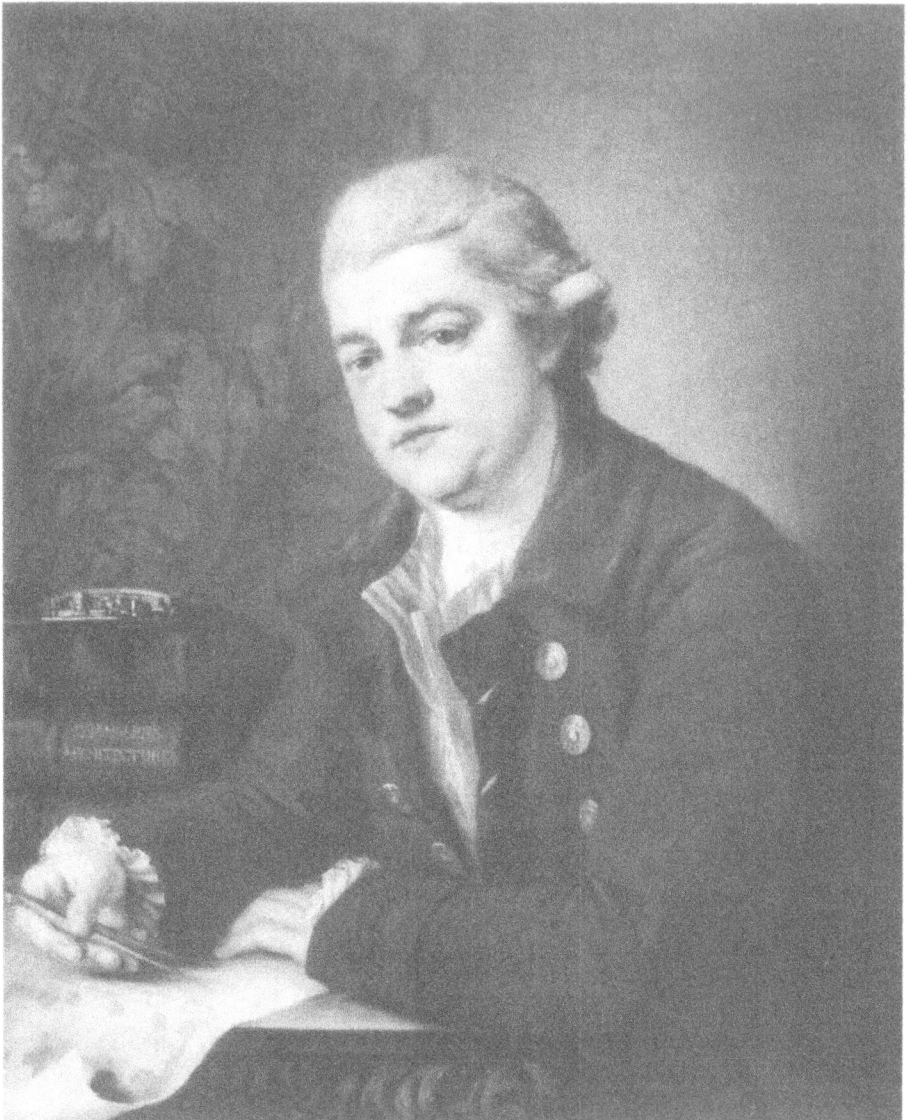

Figure 1.3 John Francis Rigaud, *John Yenn*, before 1785.
Reproduced courtesy of the Royal Academy of Arts, London, UK.

published in 1977 during the advent of the computer, for which the dust jacket, designed by Egon Lauterberg, shows a pair of isolated wing dividers, this drafting tool retained its power to represent the profession.[6] Often added to the display of an instrument were depictions of reference books, as in John Francis Rigaud's portrait from before 1785 of the Englishman John Yenn now at the Royal Academy of Arts in London (Figure 1. 3).

Yenn holds the requisite pair of dividers with its points down on a finished drawing. Just above his right hand, the one holding the dividers, are volumes on civil architecture by William Chambers, his mentor, surmounted by an open instrument case. Above that looms a sculpture of giant acanthus leaves.[7] As we shall see, the combination of instruments and books became the default position for the iconography of some architects' portraits well into the nineteenth century.

We must distinguish between compasses and dividers. The former have interchangeable legs that can hold pencils, pens, charcoal, or chalk used in making lines on paper or parchment; the latter have two pointed legs not used to draw lines but to measure (often) an existing drawing, as the important nineteenth-century English architect, "Practical Builder," and influential teacher of stair building, Peter Nicholson, demonstrates in his portrait by William Derby by holding a pair of dividers to a ruler, not to a sheet of drafting paper.[8] When dividers appear in architects' portraits, the sitter is rarely actually drawing, he is pretending to measure a finished design, or rather, merely identifying himself as an architect by showing them. But it must also be recognized that measuring is not the sole preserve of the architect, despite what Henry Hornbostel or the designer of the dust jacket of Kostof's book implied by their use of dividers to represent the profession. Cesare Ripa's *Iconologia*, an emblem book first published in 1593, for example, depicts (in the first illustrated edition of 1603) dividers in many contexts ranging from Bellezza, Disegno, and Misura to Economia, Liberalità, and Parsimonia because they all allude to the desired order and measure in all things. Dividers appear prominently in many Renaissance and Baroque (and some nineteenth-century American[9]) portraits of sitters of diverse métier. The relationship between architecture and the mathematical sciences is a close one, as we know, and there are portraits of mathematicians as well as astronomers and navigators, even musicians, holding dividers. Jan Vermeer's *Geographer* of 1699 now at the Städelsches Kunstinstitut in Frankfort holds a pair; so does the unidentified mariner in a 1624 portrait by Hendrik van der Borcht the Elder at the National Museum in Greenwich, England. Dividers frequently occur in allegorical representations of Architecture in which a woman plies the instrument (it is usually a woman although very few females could claim to be architects before the late nineteenth century[10]). There is at least one image of a woman holding a pair of dividers, however, that is neither a representation of Architecture nor a portrait of an architect. That is Maurice Quentin de

La Tour's likeness of about 1740, now in a private collection, of Émilie du Châtelet, French mathematician, physicist, and translator of Newton's *Principia Mathematica*. Many architects were shown with dividers, but it is necessary to remember that their presence in a portrait does not automatically make the sitter an architect. Nor, of course, does their absence mean the sitter is not an architect.

The use of compasses and dividers is as old as Western culture, but the relatively small compasses and dividers of the modern draftsman could only have become necessary when, in the late Middle Ages and early Renaissance, architects began to produce anticipatory design drawings on paper or parchment laid on a drafting board or table.[11] Medieval mason's used pairs of dividers to make patterns by incising lines on building stones, but that instrument was commonly much larger than the table draftsman's, as shown by an illustration in a fifteenth-century manuscript in the British Museum that depicts Euclid as a mason inscribing an architectural detail in stone with such a huge instrument.[12] When in the late Middle Ages-early Renaissance the conceiving architect appeared as an entity distinctly separate from and socially above the executing laborer within the process of building, when, that is, architecture became a liberal art and its practitioners considered to be learned gentlemen, it became desirable on the part of the architect to distinguish himself, a person who worked with his head, from the laborer, who worked with his hands (although both were assisted by tools). This division is clearly dramatized in this context in the illustrated edition of Ripa's *Iconologia*, in which *Practica* is shown as an old woman who stares downward, and thus demonstrates her restricted vision, while holding a plumb line and a large pair of mason's dividers, also pointing down. *Theorica*, on the other hand, is represented as a young woman of extended vision from whose upraised head emerges a small pair of draftsman's dividers pointing skyward as an extension of her brain (Figure 1.4).[13] In England the pioneering architect Inigo Jones was quick to appropriate the distinction between head work and hand work in his own drawings of *Theorica* and *Practica* of 1632.[14] Jones once again shows small draftsman's dividers pointing upward that seem to be extensions of Theory's brain while Practice bends to her large, downward-pointing workman's dividers and a carpenter's rule.[15] Thus did hand work and head work become differentiated iconographically in the history of building, and thus did artists and their sitters, until about the middle of the nineteenth century, often

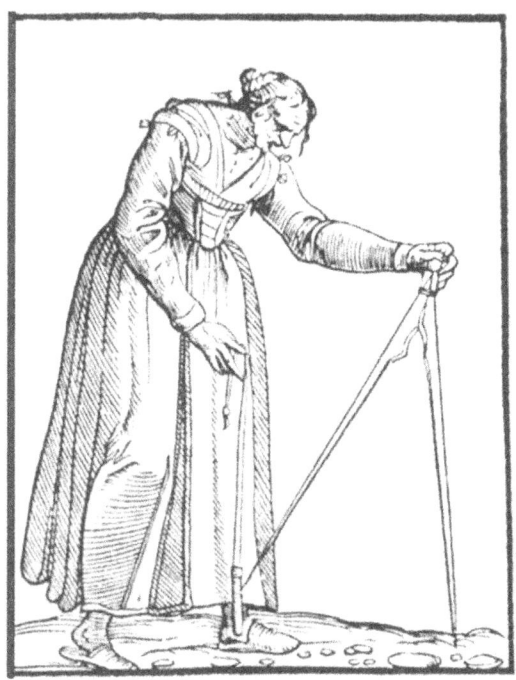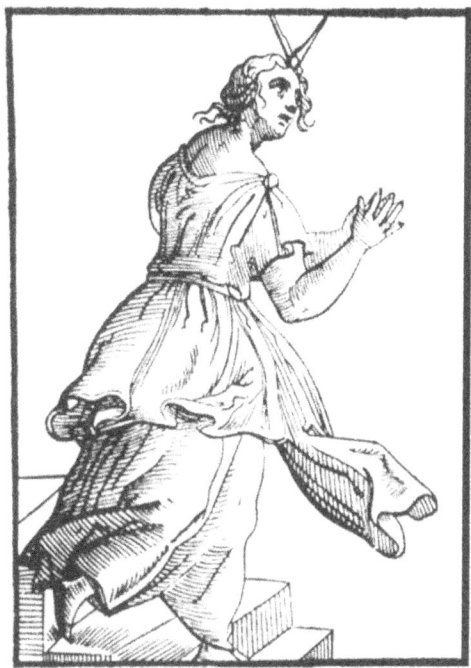

Figure 1.4 Cesare Ripa, *Theorica* and *Practica*.
Reproduced from *Iconologia overo descrittione di diverse imagini*, 1603.

appropriate draftsman's dividers as an emblem of the architect's occupation.

AMERICA

In 1774 Charles Willson Peale began a portrait of Maryland's William Buckland (1734–74) that is now in the Art Gallery at Yale University (Figure 1.5).[16] Buckland died that year and Peale finished the portrait fifteen years later at the request of the sitter's daughter. The artist (1741–1827), who studied in London with Benjamin West, was fast becoming a leading painter in the English colonies by the time this portrait was finished. Buckland had emigrated from England as an indentured carpenter and joiner twenty years earlier. Although Peale here followed in general the pattern of portraits of the English aristocracy, he adapted the pattern to a new purpose. He omitted the wig and dressy clothes shown in paintings such as that of Rigaud's *John Yenn*, but illustrated Buckland's

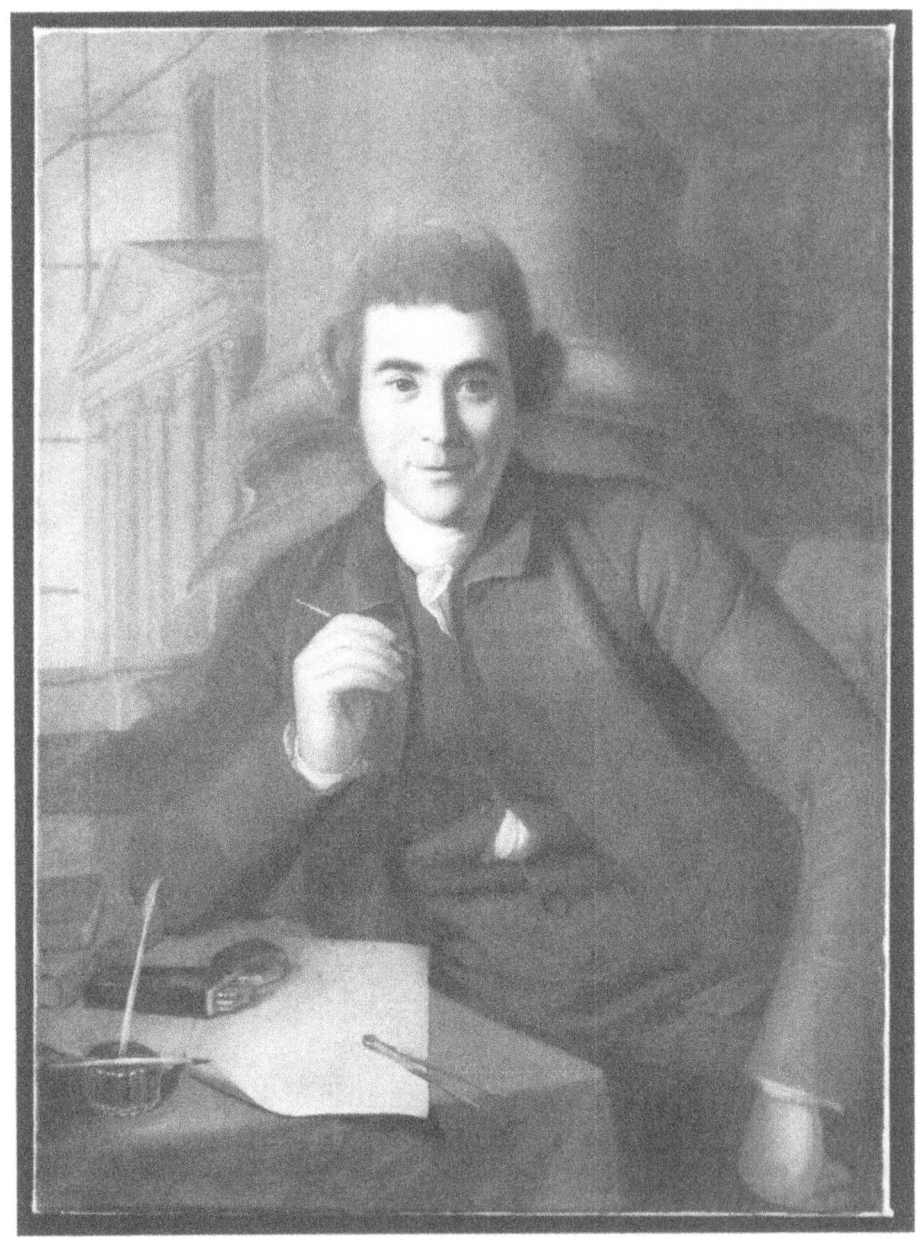

Figure 1.5 Charles Willson Peale, *William Buckland*, 1774, 1789; oil on canvas 36 ^{5}/8 x 27 ^{1}/2 in.

Reproduced courtesy of the Mabel Brady Garvan Collection, Yale University Art Gallery, New Haven, CT.

new status as the accomplished architect he had become rather than the builder he had been.[17] The sitter is alone in a room at a table covered with a green cloth drafting an unfinished design. The sheet shows plat and upright, or as we say today, plan and elevation, for what is now called the Hammond-Harwood house at Annapolis, Buckland's Georgian–Palladian masterpiece nearing completion as he sat for Peale. In the background stands an odd, five-column Corinthian portico that seems to be under construction. It is *not* part of the Hammond–Harwood house, as has been said more than once, for that building has no such unorthodox portico, and it could be a generic detail supplied by Peale long after Buckland's death, but in any event it clearly refers to Buckland's origins as a workman, a status Peale's portrait suggests he had left behind.

The drawing on Buckland's table is a far cry from modern architectural graphics. It shows no dimensions, no indication of materials, no inner-wall thicknesses, no colors, no rendering of ambience. It contains simple flat geometric diagrams of balanced classical forms drawn in black ink (perhaps over scored or pencil lines) on white (probably wove) paper.[18] Buckland's was typical of the architectural drawings of the period. He lived in an era in which the accepted standard of design stemmed from the buildings of ancient Rome as interpreted by Italian Renaissance masters such as Andrea Palladio or Giacomo Barozzi da Vignola or their English descendants, such as James Gibbs or William Chambers. And he worked in a period of traditional, largely trabeated structural technology using conventional materials such as wood and masonry. He had no need to provide elaborate graphic instructions because choices were few, and both upper-class clients and skilled builders could extrapolate from such geometrical diagrams and augment them with on-site verbal directions as necessary. Architectural drawings from the English colonies, such as what is thought to be the earliest surviving drawing, the 1732 draft, drawn on parchment, for Independence Hall attributed to Andrew Hamilton, or Thomas Jefferson's many sheets for Monticello, display the same characteristics as Buckland's for the Hammond–Harwood house.

Buckland's was surely a portrait intended for private viewing but it has much to say about the status to which the man apparently aspired. To establish his position as the creator of a building, the emerging late eighteenth- or early nineteenth-century architect primarily required two things, one of which was skill at drafting. To produce even simple diagrams, Buckland needed to know how to employ at least the basic drafting instruments, which Peale shows him plying. As we can see, Buckland possessed all the standard tools of his day housed in a typical pocket case, or etui, then available in England and its colonies, as are found, for example, in a British set from the eighteenth century now in the Andrew Alpern collection at the Avery Library, Columbia University, with its pairs of compasses and dividers, drafting pen, folding rule, scale, parallel rule, and the pocket case that contains them.[19] All were designed to produce the crisp linear graphics used by Buckland and his contemporaries. He gazes out from Peale's portrait holding upraised the drafting pen with which he has inked the lines of his drawing, proudly flaunting it, as it were, as the indication of his skill as a designing draftsman. Quill pens and an ink well sit on the table. He has pulled other tools, some of which are listed in the inventory of his estate, from the pocket case lying on the drawing. An idle pair of dividers overhangs the near edge of the table. In earlier European and British portraits the dividers usually appear more central in the composition, in accordance with Ripa's representation of *Theorica*, as we see in an ink (self?) caricature by the eighteenth-century Italian architect Carlo Marchionni, now in a private collection (Figure 1.6). Here the figure gleefully flourishes his upward-pointing measuring instrument. In contrast, what Buckland's likeness emphasizes is the ruling pen; his skill at drafting is the essential subject of the portrait. The viewer has interrupted him as he plies his instrument to record his conceptualization of the Annapolis house.

Skill at drafting would be one of the essential prerequisites of an architect in the United States, and Peale's portrait anticipates this by the prominence he gives to drawing instruments. Specialized learning would form the other necessary prerequisite. Throughout the nineteenth century, especially prior to the establishment of professional schools and large public or specialized libraries, architects relied on their own collections of reference books, or those of their gentlemen clients, for knowledge of the history of architecture, and the latest technical innovations.[20] That too is anticipated in Peale's painting by the two volumes resting on the table near the elbow of Buckland's right arm, not incidentally the arm with the hand holding the ruling pen. Books often appear in architects' portraits before 1800, as in Rigaud's *John Yenn*, or that of James Gibbs by John Michael Williams of about 1752 now in the National Portrait Gallery, London, where a book literally rather than figuratively supports a drawing that the sitter appears to measure with a pair of dividers. Buckland's volumes, like Gibbs's, assume special importance in his portrait by their placement. Peale appears to indicate that what the architect

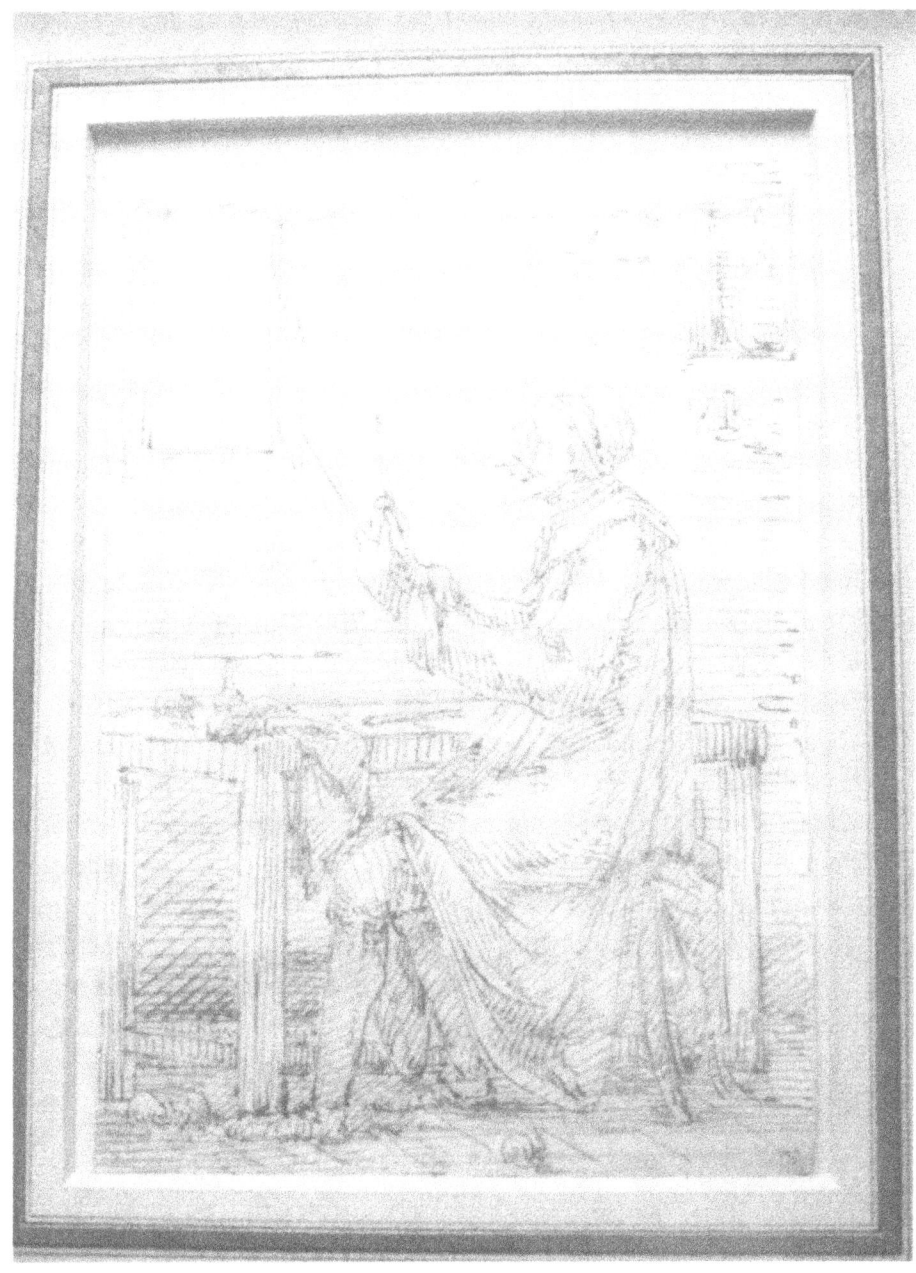

Figure 1.6 Carlo Marchionni, *Portrait of an Architect*, ca. 1750.
Private collection.

learned in the books flowed through his eyes to his brain, down his arm to his hand, into the drafting pen, and onto the paper. As was the expectation of the time, the volumes were the approved authorities, the precedents or justification for his design. Although the books in this portrait remain unidentified, the titles of more than a dozen volumes on architecture by English authors from James Gibbs to Isaac Ware appear in the inventory of Buckland's estate.[21]

Perusal of hundreds of earlier Western architects' portraits online and in the collections at Montreal and Baltimore found very few that show the subject in the act or interrupted in the act of drawing.[22] Perhaps the most cogent here is Joshua Reynolds's portrait of William Chambers now at the Royal Academy of Art in London, which bears a general compositional resemblance to Peale's *Buckland*.[23] The bewigged British architect pauses in the act of drawing with a porte-crayon in his raised hand as he works at a window through which we see his famed Somerset House in London. No other drafting tool is in evidence, but there appears to be a book on the table next to his pile of drawings. Chambers was a famous English architect; Buckland an emerging American architect. Given its historical context, Peale's portrait contains a message different from that of Reynolds's. Peale's personable sitter fixes the viewer with an intense stare as if to say: "Look at me. I have emerged from the joiner's shop to become skilled in drawing, and I now have the knowledge to prescribe my own designs as well as (or rather than) execute the ideas of others. I have moved from Practice to Theory. In the history of American building I am a new type. I am an architect." And indeed, a document of August 1773 does call Buckland an architect.[24] Such a portrait presages many others executed in the early years of the nineteenth century.[25]

NOTES

1. See Tomas B. Cole, MD, "The Cover," *Journal of the American Medical Association* 306 (17 August 2011), 684.
2. There is a pendant *Les attributs de l'artiste* in the same collection.
3. The bibliography in English on drawing instruments is headed by Maya Hambly, *Drawing Instruments 1580–1890* (London: Sotheby's Publications, 1988), followed closely by the *Catalogue of the Andrew Alpern Collection of Drawing Instruments at the Avery Architectural and Fine Arts Library* (New York: Columbia University, 2010), introduced by an essay on "Instruments, Architects, and Portraits" by the present author. That essay is an early précis of the following discussion. I correct here the misattribution and misdating there of the Renwick portrait (see below in the text) to John Ehringer (and Kenneth Hafertepe's in his *America's Castle* [Washington, DC: Smithsonian Institution Press, 1984], Figure 27).
4. In this brief Prologue I mostly focus on English and French pre-1800 paintings. For Germany and Italy see Ingrid Severin, *Baumeister und Architekten: Studien zur Darstellung eines Berufstandes in Porträt und Bildnis* (Berlin: Gebr. Mann Verlag, 1992), and Guido Beltramini and Howard Burns, *L'architetto: ruolo, volto, mito* (Venice: Marsilio Editori, 2009). For a brief characterization of European architects' portraits of the nineteenth century, see Laurent Baridon, "Les portraits d'architectes au XIXe siècle: quelle image pour quel statut?" *La revue du Musée d'Orsay* 31 (Printemps 2001), 14–23. For those of the twentieth century, see Jeffrey T. Schnapp, "The Face of the Modern Architect," *Grey Room* 33 (Fall 2008), 6–25.
5. The T-square is prominently displayed, for example, in plates in Andrea Pozzo, *Rules and Examples of Perspective* (London, Benj. Motte, 1707), a translation of his *Perspectiva pictorum et architectorum*, 1693 and 1698.
6. Simon Bosboom, *Cort onderwys van de vyf colommen . . . uyt den sherpsinnigen Vinsent Schamozzy* (Amsterdam: Frederick de Witt, 1657); Walter C. Kidney, *Henry Hornbostel* (Pittsburgh: Roberts Rinehardt, 2002), 231; Spiro Kostof, ed., *The Architect* (New York: Oxford University Press, 1977).

7. Information obtained from the records of the Royal Academy. In such earlier portraits there appears on occasion a classical column capital or other architectural fragment. These at times occur in nineteenth-century American images as well. We will notice the close proximity of dividers and books in later works.

8. Perhaps better known from the engraving by John Cochran. Because compasses have interchangeable legs, they can, of course, be easily transformed into dividers.

9. For example, Thomas Hicks's 1858 portrait of the Arctic explorer Elisha Kent Kane, New-York Historical Society, *Catalogue of American Paintings*, Part 1(New Haven, CT: Yale University Press, 1974), 414.

10. There is a gentleman in Virginia who is promoting Elizabeth Wilbraham (1632–1705) as the first woman architect on the basis of a family copy of Palladio that she annotated. There are no other documents attesting to this claim. Skeptics abound, especially concerning his assertion that Wilbraham taught Christopher Wren. This study concentrates on the images of male architects because it was not until very late in the nineteenth century (1884) that females were admitted to American architectural schools and into the drafting rooms. From the photographs of female architects posed at drafting tables or holding drafting instruments published by Sarah Allaback (*The First American Women Architects*, Chicago: University of Illinois Press, 2008), it would seem that the trajectory proposed here for portraits of men applies also to women, but begins about a century later and extends deep into the twentieth century.

11. See James S. Ackerman, "The Origins of Architectural Drawing in the Middle Ages and Renaissance," in *Origins, Imitation, Conventions: Representation in the Visual Arts* (Cambridge, Mass.: M.I.T. Press, 2002), 28–65.

12. Anthony Gerbino and Stephen Johnston, *Compass and Rule* (New Haven, CT: Yale University Press, 2009), 18: Additional MS 15692. F. 29v.

13. See Joanna Woods-Marsden, *Renaissance Self Portraiture: The Visual Construction of Identity and Social Status of the Artist* (New Haven, CT: Yale University Press, 1998), esp. 56–57.

14. Gerbino and Johnston, 66.

15. There exists at least one early portrait that seems to represent literally Ripa's *Theorica*: Jean Bernard Restout's painting of an unidentified

architect (1764) who is sometimes said to be Jacques-Germain Souf-flot now on the art market in London, who holds an open pair of dividers next to his head. For twentieth-century continuity, see El Lissitzky's representation of Vladimir Tatlin with a pair of wing dividers emerging from his eye: see Schnapp, "Face," 12.

16. Helen A. Cooper et al., eds., *Life, Liberty and the Pursuit of Happiness: American Art from the Yale University Art Gallery* (New Haven, CT: Yale University Press, 2008), 203; Lillian B. Miller, ed., *The Selected Papers of Charles Willson Peale*, volume 1 (New Haven, CT: Yale University Press, 1983) 556; and Rosamond Randall Beirne and John Henry Scarff, *William Buckland, 1734–1774* (Baltimore, MD: Maryland Historical Society, 1958.

17. For a rather different interpretation of this painting, one that made me look more closely at it, see Mary N. Woods, *From Craft to Profession* (Berkeley, CA: University of California Press, 1999), 13.

18. There is a preserved drawing of the house by Peale that closely resembles that depicted in the portrait: Beirne and Scarff, 91.

19. *Catalogue of the Andrew Alpern Collection of Drawing Instruments at the Avery Architectural and Fine Arts Library* (New York: Columbia University, 2010), 6–7.

20. See Kenneth Hafertepe and James F. O'Gorman, *American Architects and Their Books to 1848* (Amherst, Mass: University of Massachusetts Press, 2001).

21. Beirne and Scarff, 148–50. See also [Bennie Brown], "The Library of William Buckland," in *Buckland: Master Builder of the 18th Century* (Lorton, VA: Board of Regents of Gunston Hall, 1978), 27–40.

22. Two are worth mentioning: Louis-Michael van Loo's of Jacques-Germain Soufflot (1767) in the Louvre, in which the architect looks up while holding a porte-crayon with which he is meant to be seen working on an elevation of the church of Ste. Genevieve (the Panthèon) in Paris, and Pavel Andreyevitch Fedotov's of an unidenti-fied architect (ca. 1849) in the Russian Museum, St. Petersburg, in which the sitter, who smokes a cigar, looks up from his draft holding a pencil, with a set of instruments, triangle, eraser, reference book, and other bits of staffage lying about.

23. Among portraits of other types, Benjamin West's of Peale himself, 1767–69, at the New-York Historical Society, in which the sitter flaunts a porte-crayon, must also be kept in mind as precedent. Cooper, *Life, Liberty, and the Pursuit of Happiness*, 203.

24. Beirne and Scarff, 98.

25. There are several important questions to ask of such portraits: who decided on the pose and staffage? Who could have been the audience for such works? Was that audience public or private? Were portraits broadcast in reproduction? If so, where? As we shall see, there is scant evidence available to answer these questions for most of the works discussed here, although more for later likenesses. American architects' images seem to begin to appear in some kind of broadly distributed reproduction only with the beginning of monographs on architects after the Civil War. Of the first three such monographs, William W. Wheildon's *Memoir of Solomon Willard* (Boston, Mass: Monument Association, 1865), contains none; the photographic frontispiece to Edwin Martin Stone's *The Architect and Monetarian: a Brief Memoir of Thomas Alexander Tefft* (Providence, RI: Sidney S. Rider, 1869), shows the subject half-length, seated, in profile, holding a cane. These first two monographs were dedicated to men who were part-time architects. The frontispiece to Mariana Griswold Van Rensselaer's *Henry Hobson Richardson and His Works* (Boston, Mass: Houghton Mifflin, 1888) has a formal, head-and-shoulders photograph of the architect (see note 28, chapter 3, this volume). Thereafter such frontispieces become common. One might also ask how general was the use of portraits on business stationery, such as that of the 1880s by St. Louis's J. B. Legg (Woods, *From Craft to Profession,* 97). None of these can be answered in this brief introduction into the subject.

2

Portraits of the Early Nineteenth Century

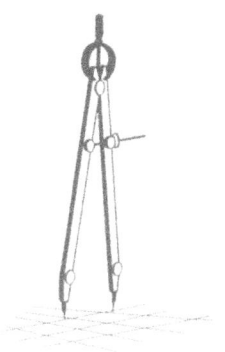

W hat follows sketches how and why the portrait of the architect in the United States during the nineteenth century evolved from Peale's three-foot tall, half-length figure of William Buckland as draftsman to John Singer Sargent's 1895, nine-foot tall, full-length likeness of Richard Morris Hunt posturing importantly at Biltmore House in North Carolina (see Figure 3.11, p. 74). We cannot consider this topic without keeping in mind the previous history of the genre, as briefly outlined in Chapter 1, as well as the evolving history of the profession. Early conditions in this country differed greatly from those of contemporary England and the Continent, but developments in the practice of architecture here in the late eighteenth and early nineteenth century recall to some extent the gradual emergence of the architect in late-medieval and early-Renaissance Europe. During the period beginning around 1800 there were very few architects as we use the term today and hence no architectural profession in the United States. Benjamin Henry Latrobe, an English immigrant, was the early, glaring exception. However, by the late nineteenth century that profession had been fully formed.[1] It is the thesis here that this development can be pictured by looking at a series of architects' portraits from that century, by putting a face, or rather faces in their settings, on that development. On the other hand, it is also the thesis here that the development of the profession accounts for the evolving iconography of the images. In a nutshell: early portraits often intentionally show staffage that normally identifies the sitter as an architect; many later portraits omit staffage in order to show the sitter as indistinguishable from other professionals. Here, so to speak, we come face to face with history.

The changing identification of type is the subject of this study. Drafting instruments and reference books were frequent identifiers of early nineteenth-century American architects, as they visually separated designer from builder, but these items were not the only ones that suggested their users were architects. Before we can turn our attention to portraits that follow (and adapt) the traditional pattern, we must make a detour to look at a few that fall into an alternate iconography. For example, John McComb, Jr. (1761–1853), codesigner (with Joseph François Mangin) of New York's City Hall of 1802–12, in a work attributed to Samuel Lovett Waldo now hanging in City Hall, is shown holding a plan, the product of his draftsmanship, that includes the astonishing rotunda of that building whose exterior appears in the background (Figure 2.1).[2] McComb was the leading architect in New York City in the first quarter

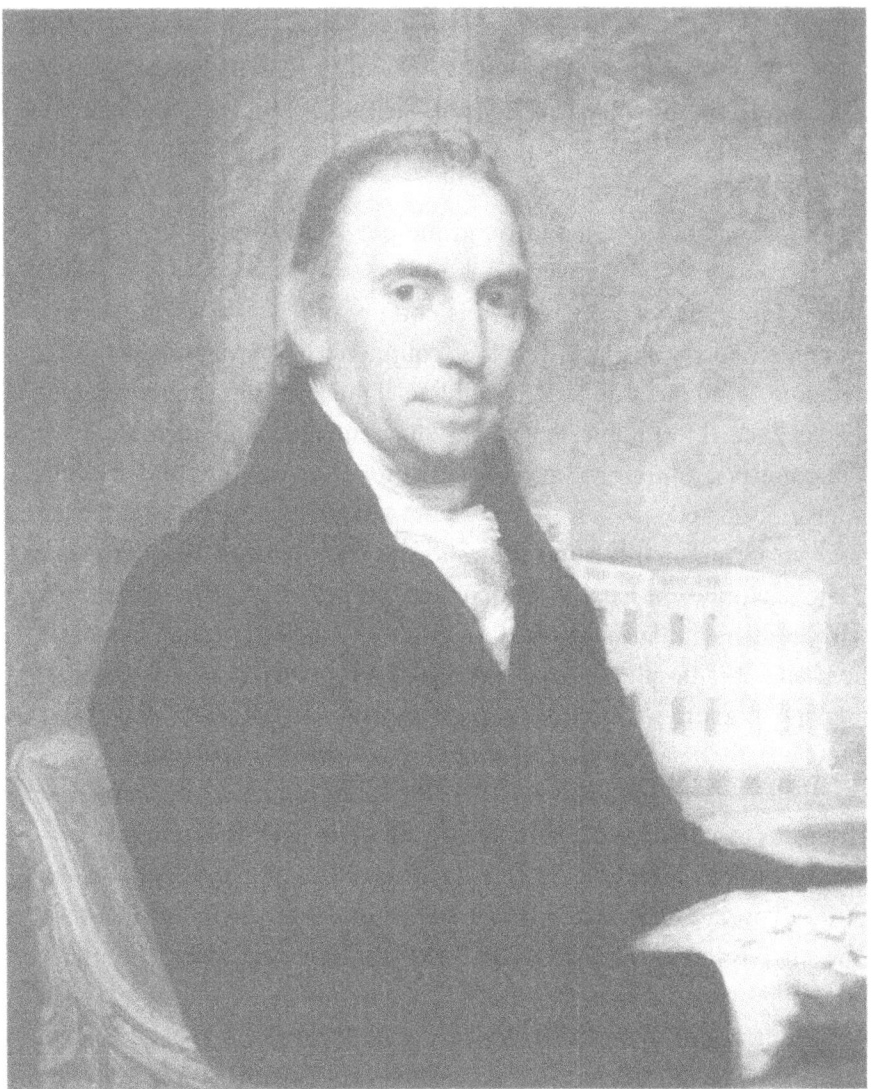

Figure 2.1   Samuel Lovett Waldo, *John McComb, Jr.*, ca. 1815; oil on canvas, 31 x 26 in. Reproduced courtesy of City Hall, New York, NY.

of the nineteenth century, and sufficiently regarded nationally by 1817 to have been considered along with Boston's Charles Bulfinch as Benjamin Henry Latrobe's successor as supervising architect of the Capitol. The portrait probably dates from the second decade of the century when McComb's career peaked. He had largely retired from practice by 1826.[3] Whether this was a private or public commission remains an unanswered question, although most likely it was private as the city acquired the work from his granddaughter in 1916. Waldo (1783–1861), who studied with Benjamin West and at the Royal Academy in London in the early years of the century, was by 1817 established as a studio portraitist in New York, as a member of the American Academy of Fine Arts, and soon to be a founder of the National Academy of Design. We find the format of this portrait—sitter, drawing, building—without visible drafting instruments, repeated through the century. A slight variation of it marks the roughly contemporary portrait of Russell Warren (1783–1860) attributed to Henry Cheever Pratt, now in the collection of the Rhode Island Historical Society.[4] When he sat to Pratt, Warren, who assumed the title of "architect" in 1828, would have been an important designer in Rhode Island, the man who created among his many works the remarkable neoclassical, granite, iron, and glass Providence Arcade of 1827–29. Pratt (1803–80), a student of Samuel F. B. Morse, was listed as a portrait painter in Providence in 1824. There is no information available about the commissioning of the painting. In the portrait, which came to the Historical Society by gift in 1916, Warren, in suit, white vest, and cravat, holds an unidentified book while seated at a table in a neoclassical interior. The table is covered with green baize on which rests a drawing of what seems to be a Corinthian capital. No building rises in the background, as it does in the McComb portrait, but a framed, rendered perspective of a Grecian prostyle, tetrastyle building hangs on the wall. It was surely intended to show off Warren's draftsmanship and showcase a generic example of his work.

Although the paintings just discussed spring from early in this study, the general format lived though the century. A special case is the posthumous portrait of James Renwick, Jr. (1818–95) at Columbia University, painted in an old-fashioned style by the sitter's cousin, Howard Crosby Renwick (active 1920s to 1940s).[5] It shows one of New York's most important mid-nineteenth-century architects holding a perspective sketch of what is probably his St. Patrick's Roman Catholic Cathedral in New York, begun in 1858, while resting his left arm on a pile of books. It is said that the portrait is based on "engravings and other data," and indeed, Renwick's head does closely follow a steel engraving by George E. Perine (1837–85). The rest of the image may have been suggested by the New York architect and historian, I. N. Phelps Stokes, who would have known earlier like portraits and was responsible for the alumni gift of this one to the university in 1929.[6] Another, more strictly nineteenth- or early twentieth-century example is the likeness of Thomas W. Richards (1836–1911) as painted by Elsa Koenig Nitzsche, probably about 1910, which is in the collection of the University of Pennsylvania. The architect, who was trained by Samuel Sloan, designed the first buildings of the university's west Philadelphia campus in the 1870s and became its first professor of architecture.[7] He is depicted holding a pencil in his right hand while resting his left on a blueprint copy of his layout of College Hall, the tower of which rises behind his right shoulder.[8] (It should be noted here that blueprints began to become common for reproducing architectural drawings about the time of the design of the university.) Elsa Koenig (1880–1952), as she was known professionally, was in her time a busy portraitist who studied with Elliot Daingerfield and in Europe.[9] Here Richards, the hoary creator of College Hall, is clearly credited with drafting its design. There was a time when the portrait hung among those of other university dignitaries in College Hall; it is now languishing in storage.[10]

Such iconography can be misleading, however. The privately owned portrait painted around 1800, perhaps also by Charles Willson Peale, of Gunning Bedford (1720–1802), a one-time president of the Carpenter's Company of Philadelphia, uses the same format.[11] He holds a line drawing of an aedicule while a round-arched portico rises in the background. Gunning was a master builder rather than an architect. At this period the distinction was not sharp, and here the format blurs the division between constructor and designer. What further confuses the issue is that the same format appears again in portraits of clients, such as Gilbert Stuart's 1824 image of Josiah Quincy at the Museum of Fine Arts, Boston, which depicts him holding the plan of the new Fanueil Hall marketplace that appears in the background. We know he did not draft the design. He was the mayor who commissioned it; Alexander Parris was the architect of the complex.

McComb's portrait (see Figure 2.1) shows him as the designer of City Hall, but this is evident only because we know he was the designer rather than, say, the mayor of New York. Following the discussion in Chapter 1, this exploration now turns to early nineteenth-century portraits that identify architects by the presence of traditional drafting instruments and/or reference books that signify their status. By mid-century different images of the architect were to emerge.

REPRESENTATION OF STATUS

By the end of the eighteenth century and the beginning of the nineteenth, with, among other developments, the rise of the Industrial Revolution and the advent of a pluralistic society in the United States, a third entity appeared between the client and the builder. This was the emerging professional architect, learned in both Ripa's *Theorica* and *Practica*, who could interpret through drawings the desires of the client and direct the work of the constructor. He was a product of the Renaissance and eighteenth-century English practice but was slow to appear in numbers on this side of the Atlantic. The Buckland portrait (see Figure 1.5, p. 10), depicting the graphic as well as the actual creation of a building, represents the predawn of architectural professionalism in this country. Its real impetus would not appear until the arrival of Benjamin Henry Latrobe at the end of the eighteenth century.

The beginning of the architectural profession in the United States embraced individuals of two different backgrounds. There were the experienced immigrants, such as Latrobe, especially from Great Britain but also from Europe, where the professional architect had been recognized for some time, and American-born men who began as carpenters, joiners, masons, and such who, like Buckland, sought to make the leap from Practice to Theory, from execution to conception, from the building site to the drafting board. Both groups encountered opposition in the United States. In the early years of the century, the emerging architect needed to emphasize the value of his contribution to the building process and the difference between that and a workman's, especially as the builder resented the architect's encroachment into his long-standing relationship with the client. The fledgling also sought to convince potential clients of his worth, clients who were not accustomed to paying for design services. These pioneering American architects needed to establish their credentials, and it would seem that some of them tried to do that in part by presenting their likenesses according to prevailing tradition, accompanied by drawing instruments and books. And, not incidentally, such a portrait could suggest a social status for an architect closer to the client than the builder.

Books on architecture, with or without accompanying drafting instruments, as signifiers of the sitter's study of the history of styles that had grown more complex with the Enlightenment and the evolving methods of construction introduced by the Industrial Revolution, occur in some portraits of nineteenth-century American architects, both early and late. In the eighteenth century those books came from abroad and mostly concerned the classical orders, but with the new century Americans began producing their own publications and these eventually included works on the picturesque styles like neo-Gothic as well. Advances in building engineering also generated new publications. The earliest native books were aimed at local builders who aspired to become architects. Among them, Owen Biddle's *The Young Carpenter's Assistant; or System of Architecture*, published in Philadelphia in 1805 is a typical work of this transitional phase.[12] The author, who describes himself as a "House Carpenter and Teacher of Architecture and Drawing," takes the mechanic by the hand and shows him how to lay out the orders. His book begins at the beginning, with instructions for making a "draught-board" and describes the kind of instruments the fledgling will need. By 1854 Boston's Edward Shaw could sum up this aspect of the early development of the profession in the title of one of his books: *The Modern Architect; or, Every Carpenter His Own Master*.[13] By mid-century it was no longer necessary for such a book to teach drawing. Shaw concentrates on the styles of architecture and the components of building. The relative position of the terms "carpenter" and "architect" in these two titles neatly captures the shift from Practice to Theory, from workman to professional, on the part of emerging American architects.

It is important to note that those architects were led by Benjamin Henry Latrobe (1764–1820), a man who represents the experienced immigrant strain in the early architectural history of the United States.[14] He was among the best-trained architects in the country after he moved from England in 1796, and certainly the most talented. A polymath like the American Ithiel Town after him, skilled in mathematics, music, a watercolorist artist, and engineer, Latrobe had studied the latest buildings of Europe, worked in the offices of the engineer John Smeaton and the architect Samuel Pepys Cockerell, both major figures, and in 1791 opened his own London practice. Latrobe was accustomed to designing, and seeing built, large complex structures as our colonial and federal builders were not. Continuing such practice with his work at the U.S. Capitol under Thomas Jefferson, Latrobe introduced highly sophisticated architectural draftsmanship for large public buildings that required not only shades and shadows suggesting space, volume, and mass, but various colored washes representing different materials.[15] These replaced the flat, monochromatic, linear diagrams of Buckland's time with attractive, easily legible drawings. He also introduced rendered anticipatory perspective views for both classical and neo-Gothic designs.[16] Architecture was now beginning to serve a clientele different from its homogenous and aristocratic past, when architecture's study was part of the education of a gentleman who could comprehend spare orthographic diagrams. A new clientele composed of the middle class or the corporate required more instructive (and seductive) graphics to explain new styles and new techniques. New building types and new building technology also required such detailed and legibly drafted instruction for the builders. With his extraordinary preparation, Latrobe came to this country surely expecting to continue to be respected in the building process, but here he ran into the lack of understanding of the value an architect had to offer. He began the process of professionalization but did not live to see it come to fruition.

Latrobe's introduction of the rendered perspective as part of the graphic process altered and enriched the drafting work of the American architect. The High Renaissance artist Raphael, channeling ancient Vitruvius and quattrocento Leon Battista Alberti, had long ago described the measured orthographic plan, section, and elevation of a building as the province of the architect, and reserved the conjuring perspective view for the artist.[17] That separation, with architects drafting flat graphics to diagram new buildings, and artists depicting standing buildings in topographical views, held more or less true in this country well into the nineteenth century, until, that is, publicists like Edward Shaw began applying the lessons we associate with Latrobe by reflecting this new trend in architectural presentation. In a book called *Civil Architecture*, first published in 1830, Shaw defended this new practice by suggesting that it was "satisfactory" and "just" for the architect to furnish the client "with views of the intended structure from different points of sight," and Philadelphia's William Strickland and John Haviland, New York's Alexander Jackson Davis, Boston's Hammatt Billings and J. G. F. Bryant, Providence's Russell Warren, the offices of peripatetic Isaiah Rogers, and others began routinely producing them. They became increasingly necessary to explain the three-dimensional result of two-dimensional plans and elevations as revived building styles changed from the ancient Roman and Greek classical orders to neo-Gothic picturesque drama, but, as we shall see, they also eventually blurred the distinction between architect and artist.

A Swedish painter active in London, Carl Frederik von Breda (1759–1818), captured Latrobe's likeness before he left England in a portrait of about 1790, now in the collection of the Maryland Historical Society in Baltimore.[18] The National Portrait Gallery at the Smithsonian Institution recently acquired a small, sketchier version of that work bearing the inscription "Mr. Latrobe" (Figure 2.2). The bewigged English architect sits at his desk staring out at the viewer, but unlike Peale's *William*

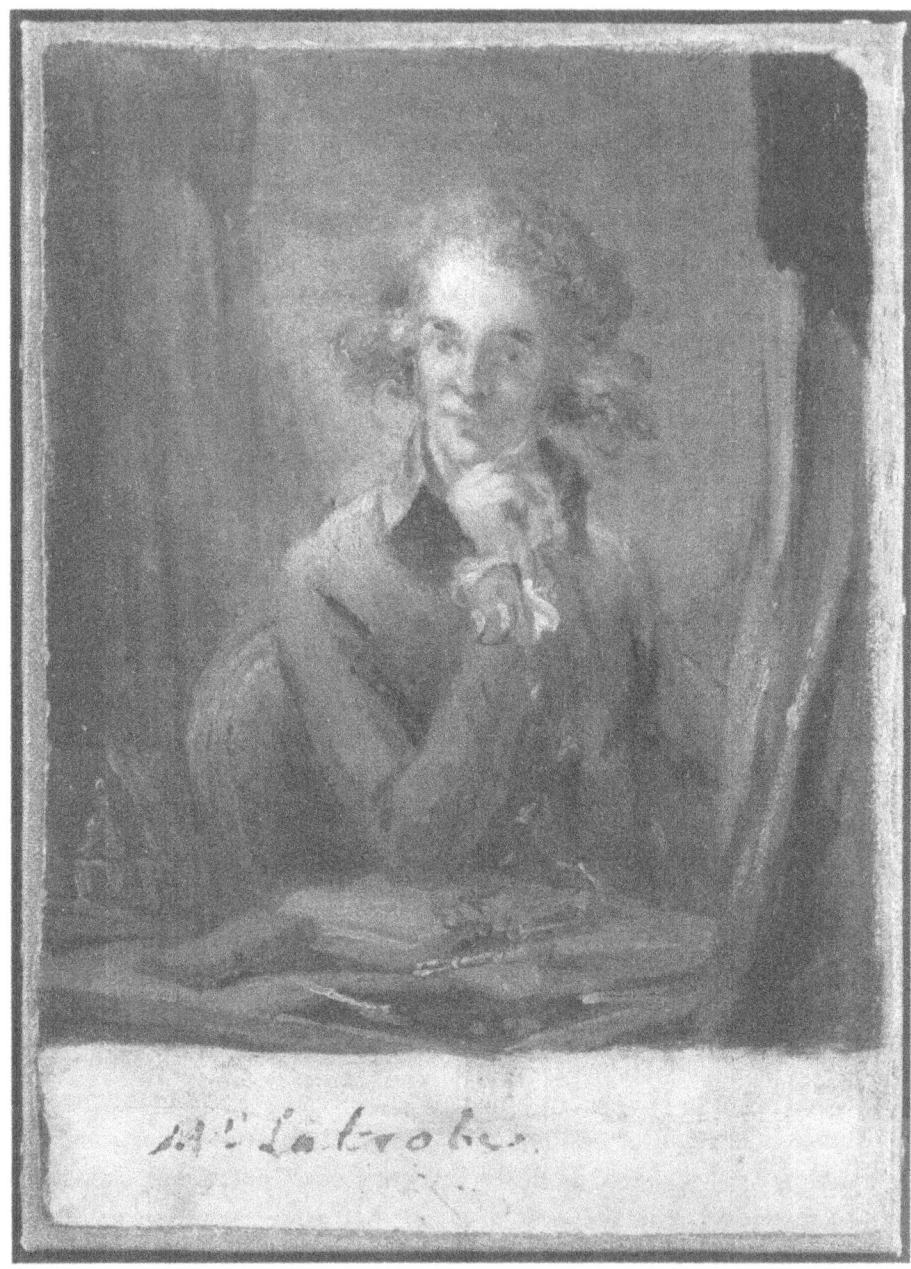

Figure 2.2 Carl Frederik von Breda, *Benjamin Henry Latrobe*, ca. 1790; oil on canvas, 7 ^{1}/$_8$ x 5 ^{1}/$_4$ in.

Reproduced courtesy of the National Portrait Gallery, Smithsonian Institution, Washington, DC.

Buckland, he is not drawing. His head is propped on his right hand in the common representation of a thinker, one who works with his brain. He has about him the careless air of the aristocrat. On the desk are haphazardly strewn the idle tools of his world: books, porte-crayon, drawings, portfolios, dividers, quill pen, perhaps some gold coins, and a pair of spectacles. This rather messy assortment nonchalantly captures the needs of the draftsman in a way somewhat distant from the bulk of contemporary English architects' portraits, with their neat combination of books and dividers. After some years of often frustrating attempts to establish architecture as a viable profession in the minds of clients and builders in the United States, Latrobe sought to have his portrait painted in his new country, this time by Gilbert Stuart, whom he called "the greatest painter we have ever seen." In 1805 he erected a "painting room" on land Stuart had leased in Washington, and tried to help the artist, who was at that point ill and destitute, but failed. "I could do nothing with him," the architect wrote, "not even get him to paint my own portrait, — which, if he ever paints it, will cost me 1000 dollars, & more."[19] Such a portrait may have been executed at a later date, however, about 1810 or so, for there exists in a private collection in Philadelphia a likeness said to be of Latrobe of about that date or slightly later attributed to Stuart (1755–1828). In this work the sitter is wigless and shown more traditionally than in the Von Breda likeness with a book, a pair of dividers in his right hand, and a rolled set of drawings in his left. A tassel hanging from the rear curtain mimics the form of the federal Capitol presumably as Latrobe conceived it.[20] This second image is more in line with what we would expect in an American architect's portrait of this period, one that follows closely what we have identified as a prevailing iconography of such works. If this is indeed Latrobe (and who else could it be?), his career of frustration trying to establish himself as a professional architect in the States demonstrates that he as well as the aspirant local carpenters wanted to be portrayed with the recognized attributes of that status.

Hewing closer to traditional representation of an architect than Von Breda's portrait of Latrobe, but also incorporating signs of the new era, is John Neagle's 1828 likeness of another British immigrant, John Haviland (1792–1852), now at the Metropolitan Museum of Art in New York (Figure 2.3). The sitter apprenticed in London with James Elmes, an architect whose work shows reliance on the standard source of the Greek Revival, Stuart and Revett's multivolume work on the antiquities of Athens. Haviland arrived in Philadelphia in 1816, lectured and taught drafting

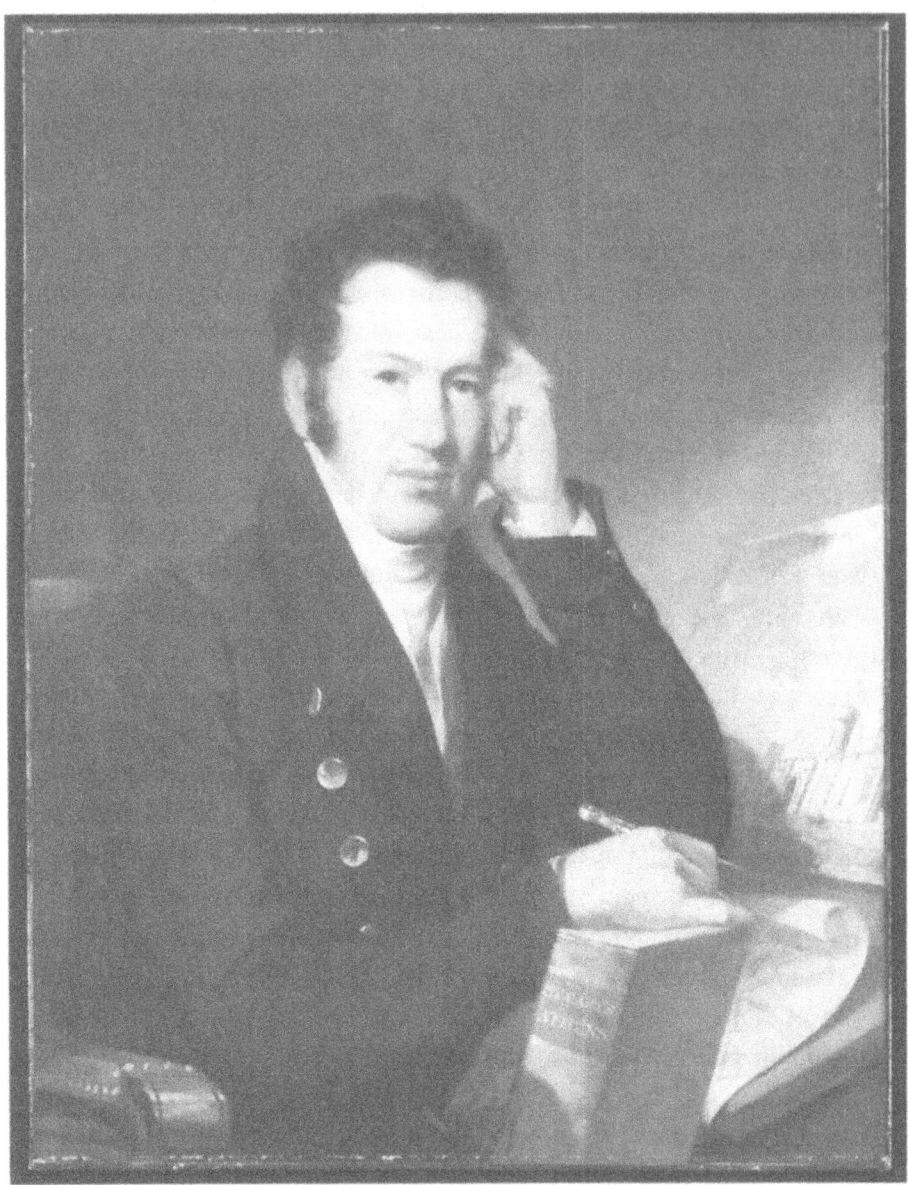

Figure 2.3   John Neagle, *John Haviland*, 1828; oil on canvas, 33 x 26 in.
Reproduced courtesy of the Metropolitan Museum of Art–Art Resource, New York, NY.

in the city, published with Hugh Bridport a work with the then characteristic title of *The Builder's Assistant* (1818–21), moved into a period of prosperity in the 1820s, then gradually faded from attention.[21] Neagle (1796–1865), like his brother-in-law Thomas Sully, was an active portraitist in Philadelphia from the 1820s on.[22] He posed the architect—or the architect posed himself, we do not know the circumstances of the commissioning—at a table thrusting toward the viewer one volume of Stuart and Revett. Haviland steadies the book with his right hand while grasping the traditional pair of dividers—thus tightly linking book and instrument—while the index finger of his left hand points to his brain. This not only reflects the standard type of portraiture for architects that we saw in Chapter 1, it also recalls works such as John Singleton Copley's 1768 likeness of Paul Revere at the Museum of Fine Arts in Boston, in which the silversmith holds an example of his craftsmanship in one hand and his head in the other. These are clearly visual references to the sitters' occupations as requiring, as the Massachusetts Institute of Technology's motto would have it, both *mens* and *manus*, both mental and manual effort. Haviland's pointing to his brain emphasizes Ripa's *Theorica*, and must have been intended to show him as a skilled, knowledgeable, and thoughtful designer who plied reference books as well as drafting instruments in the production of his buildings.

To the left of the sitter there is a plan and a perspective view of Haviland's masterpiece, the internationally regarded, castellated, Eastern State Penitentiary in Philadelphia, designed in 1821. The perspective from his hand makes visible the up-to-date stylistic range of his thinking, and demonstrates that he was not limited to classical precedent, that the architect's sources had been greatly augmented since the previous century. The colored perspective view (like that hung on the wall, as we have seen, in a roughly contemporary portrait of Russell Warren) shows the influence in America of the British training Haviland shared with Latrobe, and a marked advance over William Buckland's Hammond–Harwood draft. And where Peale included a view of a construction site, perhaps in reference to Buckland's origins as a builder, here there is a presentation drawing probably intended for the client. As Lois Price so well puts it in her book on the fabrication and conservation of architectural drawings, by this time "the ability to produce sophisticated architectural renderings informed by a thorough familiarity with architectural history and current styles became a defining attribute of the architectural profession."[23]

Although he began as a carpenter, native-born Ithiel Town (1784–1844) of New Haven and New York was hardly typical of the early rank and file of emerging home-grown architects because he evolved into one of the most important men in the history of the formation of the profession in this country. Town, designer, bridge engineer, mathematician, partner of Alexander Jackson Davis in the first architectural firm in the county, and one of the five founders of the Architectural Library of Boston in 1809,[24] is nonetheless perhaps most famous as the proprietor of a private collection said to have contained 11,000 books and 25,000 prints on the history of art and architecture, a collection then unrivaled in the United States. As he freely opened his library to anyone who would profit from its contents, knowledge of the history of architecture radiated outward from his home and office.[25] In 1836 he was made an honorary and corresponding member of the Royal Society of British Architects (RIBA) in London. At least one of his portraits updates Buckland's as a declaration of having arrived, and then some.

Two important likenesses of Town exist. In the one attributed to his friend Nathaniel Jocelyn (1796–81), now at the National Academy of Design in New York where it was customary for members to donate a painting when elected to membership, the architect sits at a table fingering the pages of an illuminated manuscript bound with metal clasps, while beyond the window at the rear appears part of a hill topped by a Grecian Doric colonnade.[26] The multi-talented Jocelyn visited Europe with Town in 1829–30, then devoted himself, among other interests, to engraving and portrait painting in New Haven and New York.[27] This visual reference to Town's achievements as Greek Revival architect and dedicated bibliophile is greatly expanded in a second portrait, now the property of the Center Church on the Green in New Haven, signed and dated 1839 by Frederick R. Spencer (1806–75).[28] No information about its commissioning is known to have survived. The artist studied at the National Academy of Design and eventually became a member. He worked in New York as a portrait and genre painter until he retired in 1858. In this portrait the iconography is complex, and the painting hangs in such a location and is in such a condition that an assured complete description of its contents is not at present possible (Figure 2.4). The architect, some fifty-five years old at the date of the painting, sits at his desk holding what looks like a pen but might be a stylus or pricker surrounded by mementos of his distinguished career. At lower left a portfolio leans against his chair. Over his right shoulder are tomes taken from his library, a volume of Nicholas Revett's *The Antiquities of Ionia* (1769–97), what looks like a volume of Stuart and Revett's *Antiquities of Athens* (1762–87), and apparently a Bible. To his left on the desk a sheet of Euclidian diagrams leans against more books, one closed with clasps, an open medieval hymnal or book of Psalms, and an etui with drawing instruments lying on top

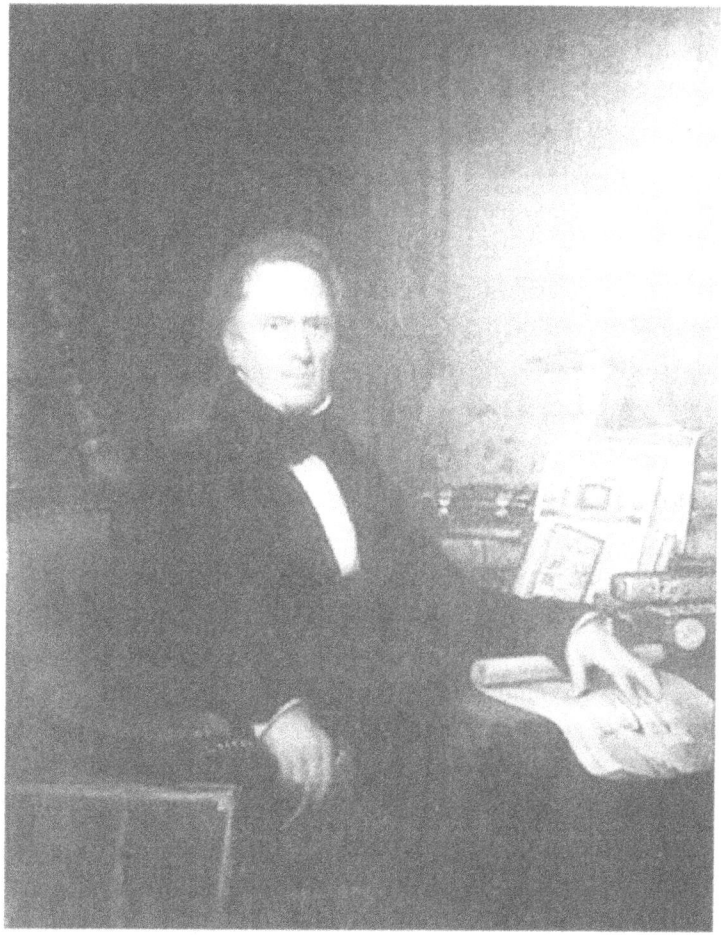

Figure 2.4   Frederick R. Spencer, *Ithiel Town*, 1839; oil on canvas, 48 x 40 in. Reproduced courtesy of Center Church, New Haven, CT.

of another, flat, instrument case.[29] Prominently located is a circular medallion said to display the image of St. George slaying the dragon.[30] Above the hymnal a one-point perspective shows the Grecian Doric distyle in antae portal to a receding covered bridge erected in 1839 using Town's patented (1820) lattice truss, the source of his wealth. His left hand rests on a scrolled illustration of a "Bridge and Aqueduct [erected on the] Principle of I. Town." This assemblage of objects seems to favor Town's scientific and bibliophilic accomplishments over his architecture, but he was more of a polymath than most of his professional contemporaries and perhaps wanted to point up that distinction.[31] As R. W. Liscomb has written, such a portrait depicts Town as "the equal of the dilettanti and antiquarian artists and architects whom he had met in London and on the continent."[32] This represented a major step up in status beyond earlier American architects' portraits.

In their portraits, architects might show off their books, imported and native, with or without instruments, as does Jocelyn's of Town. We have noted the (unidentifiable) volume held by Russell Warren in Pratt's portrait. The ca. 1806 likeness of Thomas Dawes (1731–1809), a Boston mason turned patriot turned architect, was probably commissioned by him or his family. Attributed to Gilbert Stuart (1755–1828), the acclaimed portraitist of the period, and now in the collection of Historic New England in Boston, it shows him proudly holding a book labeled simply "Palladio." Although Dawes owned the sixth edition (1700) of Godffrey Richards's translation of Palladio's first book, this probably represents William Salmon's *Palladio Londinensis: or, The London Art of Building* originally published in 1734, a builder's guide Dawes also owned and apparently favored.[33] The artist had no room on the spine of the book to include the whole of that title, but leaving off all but Palladio's name also made it seem as if Dawes owned and studied a work by the influential sixteenth-century Italian master himself, and that certainly helped to enhance his image.[34] Why he chose not to allude to his drafting skills, demonstrated in surviving drawings, remains unexplained, although it might anticipate the same reluctance by later architects for the same reason, as we shall see, that in his portrait a gentleman might hold a book but not a tool. Royall Brewster Smith's 1840 likeness of the otherwise unknown Edwin Pierce (1801–55), perhaps like the artist a resident of Maine, is also at Historic New England. It seems to identify Pierce's occupation as the book he shows the viewer is labeled on its spine simply "Architect."[35] No drafting instrument is in evidence here, either. A sitter holding a book could be anyone—a preacher with a Bible, for instance. Jocelyn's *Ithiel Town* identifies Town by the temple in the background (although we have seen that builders and clients are also shown thusly at times). We know Dawes and Pierce were architects because of what is written on their books. The combination of books *and* drafting instruments remained the most reliable iconography for the portrait of an architect in this early period.

FROM CANVAS TO PHOTOGRAPH

Not every architect could aspire to a painted portrait. With the introduction of Daguerre's invention to the United States by the painter Samuel

F. B. Morse in 1839, by the 1840s portraiture no longer need be confined to oil on canvas, and hence became more economically affordable to men who emerged from the building trades. About the same time that the native New Hampshire self-educated carpenter-turned-architect Aaron Morse (1806–49) advertised in the 1844 Concord directory that he made "Drafts of every description . . . for others to execute," thus distancing himself from the construction site, he visited a daguerreotypist's studio (Figure 2.5).[36] The resulting portrait proudly displays the signifiers of his newly adopted occupation on a table draped with a patterned rug: an open book (which remains unidentified although it seems to show an engineering diagram) and a flat case of drawing instruments containing pairs of compasses and dividers, scale, parallel rule, eraser holder, protractor, and so on. As we have seen, the shift of status from mechanic to architect began with the builder collecting books, learning to use the instruments of design, and making such accomplishments known. This would have been especially necessary in rural areas. In this period, more visible urban architects such as Henry Austin of New Haven—a builder-turned-architect—and Alexander Jackson Davis in New York—an artist-turned-architect—were publishing newspaper advertisements of their services that emphasized their libraries and their drawings.[37] Morse's portrait heralds the appearance of photography as a new, popular medium for some architects' portraits, and seems to take on the characteristics of advertising by a fledgling professional, although it is hard to imagine how such a small, unique object might have been used to promote his services.[38] It might be said that such images were made to confirm his status to the sitter and his family.

Aaron Morse was not alone in employing Daguerre's process to capture his qualifications through staffage. Such portraits or "occupational poses" as they are called by collectors, were a common product of the daguerreotypists. The patterned rug covering the table in the Morse likeness, replacing the green baize of Buckland's earlier portrait, must have been standard among architects of the mid-nineteenth century, for it appears often in such images, as in a daguerreotype now at the Canadian Centre for Architecture at Montreal in which an unidentified draftsman, whom the viewer has interrupted, sits at such a rug-covered table plying his pen while displaying his instruments spread on his paper or in a flat case. Propped against the wall is probably his own perspective drawing of a church in the then fashionable neo-Gothic style. Another half-plate image, recently at auction, also shows an unnamed architect at work,

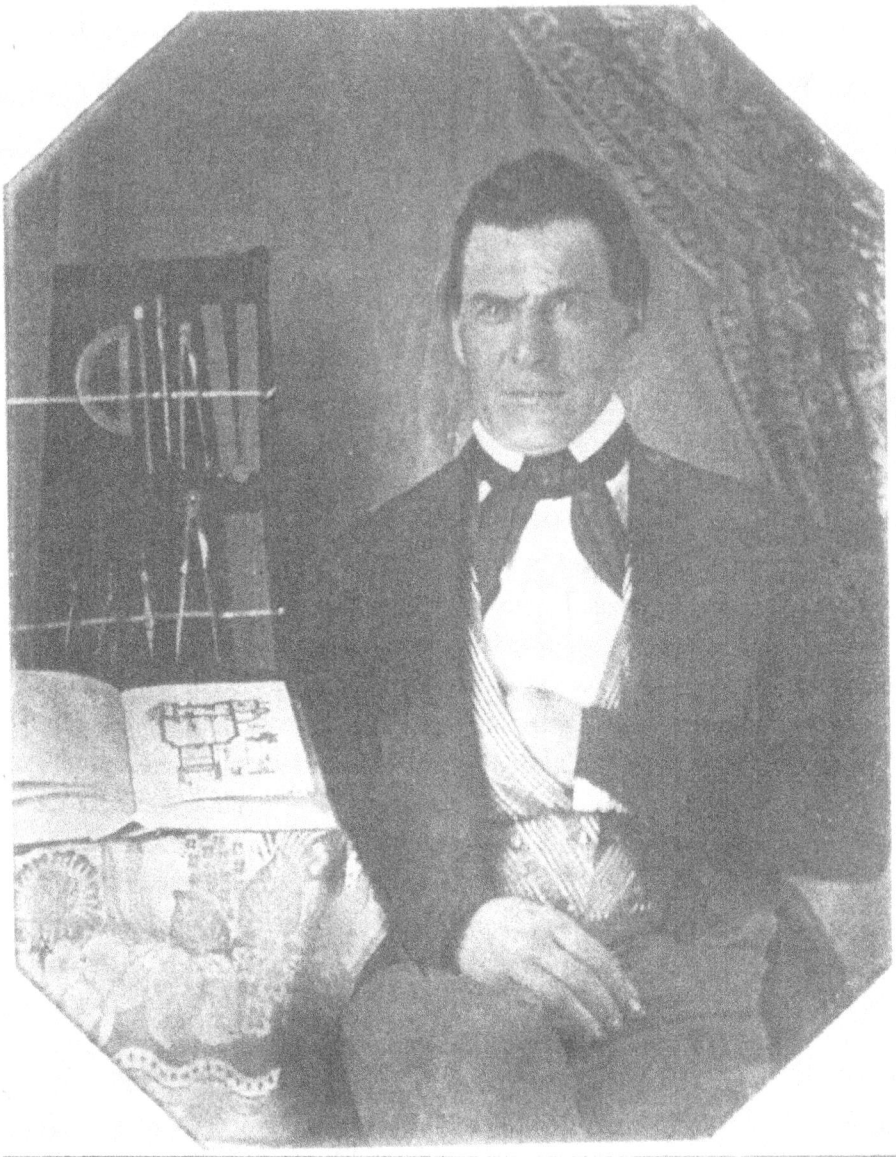

Figure 2.5 Unknown daguerreotypist, *Aaron Morse*, ca. 1848.
Reproduced courtesy of the Collection of William H. Skerritt.

his instruments scattered on his drafting table, a couple of what are probably his drawings, and plates (including designs XXVI and XXXVII) pulled from William Ranlett's publication, *The Architect* of 1847–48, an American pattern book. This was certainly to suggest that the work he turned out was up-to-date and thoroughly researched. The unknown sitter thus demonstrated his home-grown and *au courant* sources of inspiration.[39]

THE ARCHITECT AS ARTIST

Artistic developments in the character of architectural drawing introduced by immigrants such as Latrobe and Haviland slowly seeped into architectural offices in the early nineteenth century. Under their influence, Philadelphia's native-born designers led the way. Early on the new direction appeared in the portrait of William Strickland (ca. 1787–1854), who stands before his early Grecian masterpiece, the Second Bank of the United States of 1818–24, in John Neagle's portrait, signed and dated 1829, now at the Art Gallery of Yale University (Figure 2.6). Again the origins and intended destination of the painting remain unknown. Strickland had been trained as a mason, but the bank behind him is clearly not under construction.[40] Close inspection of the canvas reveals that the building is rendered with draftsman-like linear precision, whereas the figure of the sitter has a brushy, painterly appearance. Could the background have been given to the architect to execute while the likeness was Neagle's work? In any event, by the time of this portrait Strickland had become a gifted architect and accomplished perspectivist and, appropriately here, grasps a drawing board and a porte-crayon holding a brush or a piece of sharpened charcoal.[41] This portrait illustrates the appearance of an architect who uses the flexible tools of the artist in addition to the rigid tools of the draftsman.

Strickland's portrait points to things to come in architects' offices. Although he himself emerged from construction sheds to become an artist-architect, there were others who never dirtied their hands at a building site, and in that anticipated a characteristic of later architects. One of the most important architects and perspectivists of his era, Alexander Jackson Davis (1803–92), Ithiel Town's erstwhile partner, thought of himself as an "architectural composer."[42] He was the foremost renderer of topographical views but also projected picturesque Gothic villas, illustrating, for example, the popular publications of Andrew Jackson Downing on domestic architecture.[43] The rendered perspective by an architect soon became viewed as a work of art intended for public display, and hence as bait to catch a client. Davis showed his drawings at the American Academy of the Fine Arts and the National Academy of Design in New

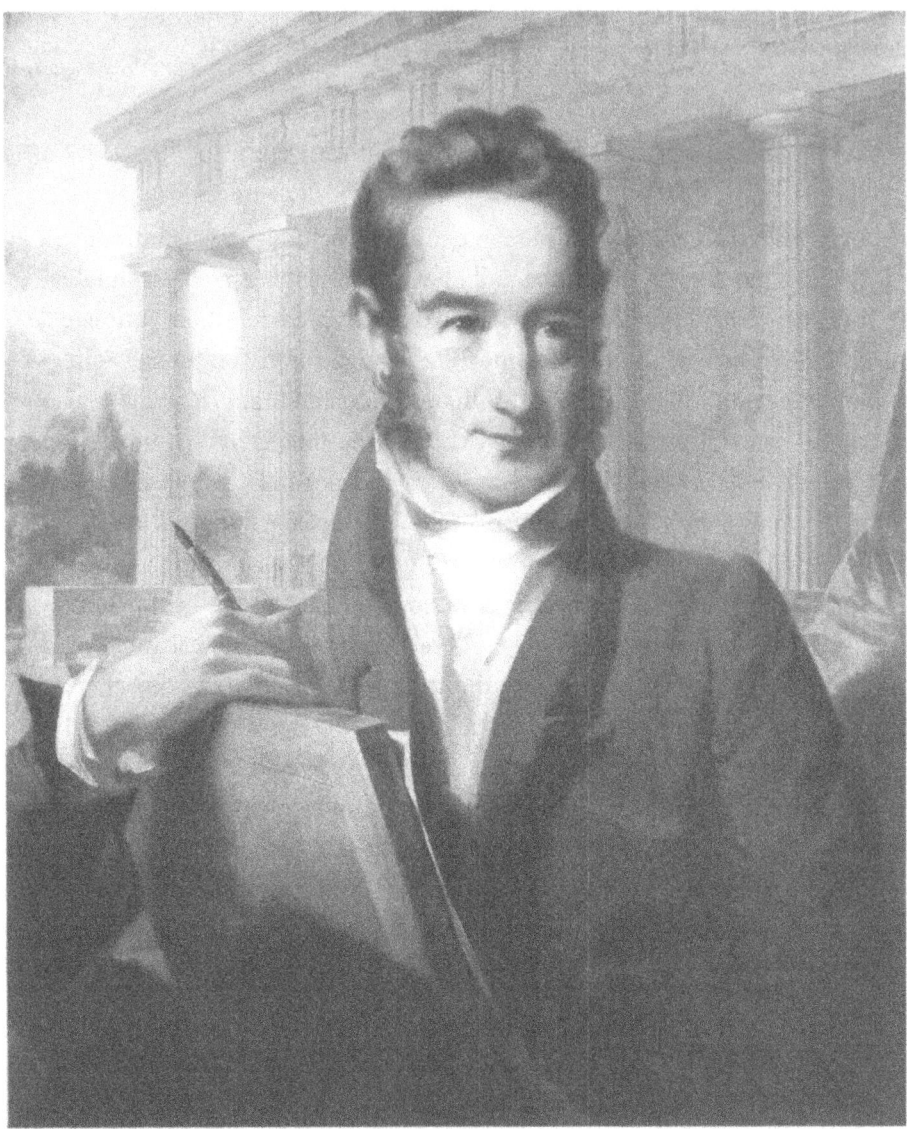

Figure 2.6 John Neagle, *William Strickland*, 1829; oil on canvas, 30 x 25 in.
Reproduced courtesy of the Mabel Brady Garvin Collection, Yale University Art Gallery, New Haven, CT.

York as early as the 1820s. Many such drawings, by Davis and others, were widely circulated as colored lithographs. The beginning of the public's view of the architect as an artist rather than a mere draftsman or builder dates to just after the period in which Neagle painted the portrait of Strickland. Unlike the carpenters- or masons-turned-architects of these early years, the lives of men like Davis or Hammatt Billings

38

(1818–74) of Boston, who with his brother Joseph designed, among many other works, the Boston Theater and the original building of Wellesley College (1869–75), represent a different career track, as artist-architects. Billings was as much a book illustrator as architect, providing the original pictures for William Bailey Lang's Downingesque *Views . . . of the Highland Cottages at Roxbury* (1845) as well as those in *Uncle Tom's Cabin* (1852), and hundreds of other books.[44] Mary Freeman Goldbeck (b. 1817), a New York poet and "talented" painter, pictured this kind of architect when she sketched Davis not with books and dividers or posed before one of his buildings, but leafing through what appears to be a portfolio of his drawings in a mid-century pencil likeness now at the Avery Library at Columbia University.[45] Although hardly an official portrait, it captures a central aspect of Davis's career.

The artist-architect survived far beyond mid-century. An editorial in *The American Architect and Builders' Monthly* for March 1870 "defined the architect as an artist."[46] In portraiture, the presentation of this status came to full flower (to anticipate the next section of this discourse) in works such as an obviously posed photograph of about 1880 of Philadelphia's George Wattson Hewitt (1841–1916) now in a private collection. Because he was himself a skilled and innovative photographer, this could be a self-portrait (Figure 2.7). Hewitt, who had apprenticed with John Notman and briefly joined Frank Furness in partnership (they designed the Pennsylvania Academy of the Fine Arts in 1871), sits at a table holding aloft not a drafting pen as does Peale's Buckland, nor a pair of dividers as does Carlo Marchionni in his caricature of an architect, but an artist's brush, as he pauses in the act of painting a watercolor, perhaps a presentation perspective of a house or other building. His set of pigments and a water glass rest on the table. None of the traditional drafting tools, those instruments of sharp, linear, black-and-white diagrams, is in evidence. The impetus to produce rendered presentation drawings reaches back in this country through Strickland to Latrobe, but this portrait stems from a period in which architects became known as artists, praised for routinely turning out "jaunty little perspective sketches" with which to impress a client, as Philadelphia's Benjamin Linfoot wrote in his appropriately titled book, *Architectural Picture Making*, of 1884. The image of the architect had merged with that of the artist, and Hewitt surely intended this photograph to convey that message. He was not alone.

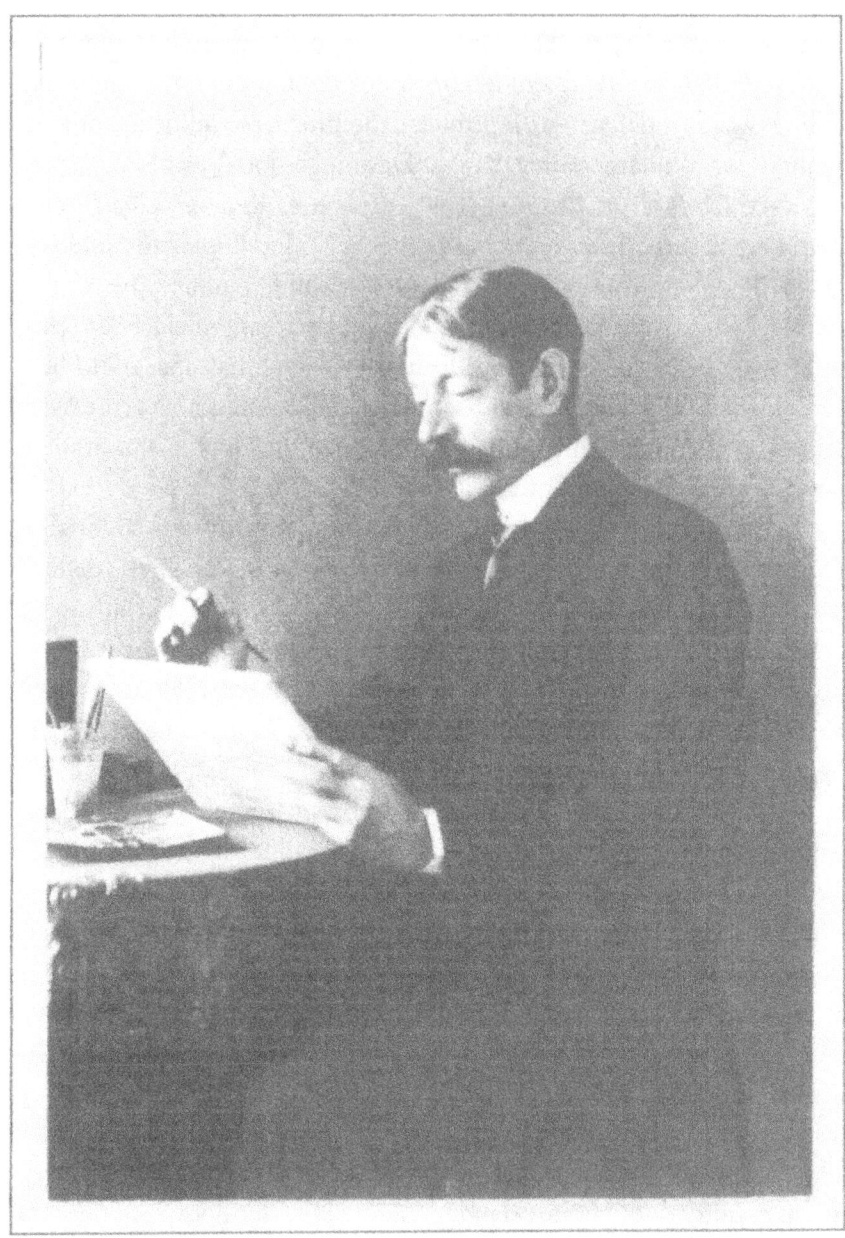

Figure 2.7 Self-portrait (?), *George Wattson Hewitt*, photograph, ca. 1880.
Private collection.

NOTES

1. The definitive study is found in Mary N. Woods, *From Craft to Profession* (Berkeley, CA: University of California Press, 1999). I have learned much from this well-documented survey. See also Andrew Saint, "The Architect as Businessman: The United States in the Nineteenth Century, in *The Image of the Architect* (New Haven, CT: Yale University Press, 1983). The architect as businessman rather than gentleman is a particularly American development, at least in the eyes of Englishmen. See note 35, Chapter 3, this volume.

2. Edith Gaines, "Portraits in New York's City Hall," *Magazine Antiques* (October 1961), 346.

3. Damie Stillman, "Artistry and Skill in the Architecture of John McComb, Jr." (master's thesis, University of Delaware, 1956); Damie Stillman, "New York City Hall: Competition and Execution," *Journal of the Society of Architectural Historians* 23 (October 1964), 129–142.

4. The online file of the Rhode Island Historical Society reproduces the painting and dates ca. 1824. *Russell Warren in Coastal Towns of Southeastern New England* (ex. cat.: The Gallery of Southeastern New England, 1982) gives ca. 1845. I favor the earlier date. See also Robert Alexander, "The Architecture of Russell Warren," (master's thesis, New York University, 1952).

5. The painting is reproduced (although misattributed to John W. Ehringer) in Kenneth Hafertepe, *America's Castle* (Washington, D C: Smithsonian Institution, 1984), 101. The elusive Howard Crosby Renwick was born in 1885. Under the name Hayden Hayden he was a busy illustrator and painter of glamour girls and pinups, according to online information.

6. Information about this painting comes from the files of the Office of Art Properties at Columbia University. Stokes himself is depicted in a portrait of 1930 by DeWitt M. Lockman now at the New-York Historical Society. In the portrait Stokes is surrounded by a book, a classical torso, and papers alluding to his interests in literature, art, and history: *Catalogue of Portraits*, Part 2, 767. (There is a fine

unrelated portrait head of Renwick by Thomas Hicks dated 1863 in the archive of the Century Club, New York.)

7. Ann L. Strong and George E. Thomas, *The Book of the School: The Graduate School of Fine Arts of the University of Pennsylvania* (Philadelphia: The Authors, 1990), 13–17.

8. "University Receives Two Portraits," *The Pennsylvania Gazette* (November 21, 1919), 206.

9. *Evening Public Ledger* (Philadelphia), 14 July 1915, 8, with illustration.

10. See note 44, Chapter 3, this volume.

11. Illustrated in James F. O'Gorman et al., *Drawing Toward Building: Philadelphia Architectural Graphics, 1732–1986* (Philadelphia: University of Pennsylvania Press, 1986), 3. A full-size photographic reproduction hangs in Carpenters' Hall, Philadelphia; the original remains in a private collection.

12. Michael J. Lewis, "Owen Biddle and *The Young Carpenter's Assistant,*" in *American Architects and Their Books to 1848*, eds. Kenneth Hafertepe and James F. O'Gorman (Amherst, Mass: University of Massachusetts Press, 2001), 149–62.

13. Edward Shaw, *The Modern Architect*, Introduction by Earle G. Shettleworth, Jr. (New York: Dover Publications, 1995).

14. See Talbot Hamlin, *Benjamin Henry Latrobe* (New York: Oxford University Press), 1955.

15. See Jeffrey A. Cohen and Charles E. Brownell, *The Architectural Drawings of Benjamin Henry Latrobe* (New Haven, CT: Yale University Press, 1994).

16. See James F. O'Gorman, *The Perspective of Anglo-American Architecture* (Philadelphia: The Athenaeum, 1995).

17. Vincenzo Golzio, *Raffaello nei documenti* (Westmead, Farnborough, Hants, UK: Gregg International Publishers, 1971), 89–90. First published 1936.

18. Emil Hultmark, *Carl Frederik von Breda, sein Leben und sein Schaffen* (Stockholm: Centraltryckeriet, 1915), 132.

19. Hamlin, *Latrobe*, 315–17.

20. I have not seen this privately owned portrait. My inadequate description comes from the listing in the Art Inventories Catalog of the Smithsonian American Art Museum and a grey Polaroid image supplied by the Smithsonian. It is not listed in Carrie Rebora Barratt and Ellen G. Miles, *Gilbert Stuart* (New Haven, CT: Yale University

Press, 2004), but that is not a *catalogue raisonné*. I do not know the documentation for the identification of the sitter or the artist. To compare the features of the sitter in this portrait with those near contemporary ones of Latrobe by the Peales is to find differences, not surprisingly, but it is hard to think of who else it might be.

21. See Matthew Baigell, "John Haviland." Ph.D. diss., University of Pennsylvania, 1965; and idem, "John Haviland in Philadelphia, 1818–1826," *Journal of the Society of Architectural Historians* 25 (October 1966), 197–208.

22. Robert Wilson Torchia, *John Neagle, Philadelphia Portrait Painter* (Philadelphia, PA: Pennsylvania Historical Society, 1989). This catalogues only locally owned paintings, so Yale's *Haviland* is not discussed.

23. See Lois Olcott Price, *Line, Shade and Shadow: The Fabrication and Preservation of Architectural Drawings* (New Castle, Del.: Oak Knoll Press, 2010).

24. Martha J. McNamara, "Defining the Profession: Books, Libraries, and Architects," in *American Architects and Their Books to 1848*, eds. Hafertepe and O'Gorman, 73–89.

25. See Roger Hale Newton, *Town & Davis, Architects* (New York: Columbia University Press, 1942); Sarah Allaback, "Louisa Tuthill, Ithiel Town, and the Beginnings of Architectural History Writing in America," in *American Architects and Their Books to 1848*, eds. Hafertepe and O'Gorman, 199–215; R. W. Liscombe, "A 'New Era in My Life': Ithiel Town Abroad," *Journal of the Society of Architectural Historians* 50 (March 1991), 5–17.

26. David B. Dearinger, ed., *Paintings and Sculpture in the Collection of the National Academy of Design*, vol. 1, 1826–1925 (New York: Hudson Hills Press, 2004), 319. The NAD gives no date; the Art Inventories Catalogue of the Smithsonian Institution gives ca. 1835; Liscomb, "New Era," 9, gives 1824, which seems too early. There is a ca. 1910 copy of the portrait by Herman Sodersten at the New Haven Museum according to the Smithsonian Art Inventories Catalogue.

27. Dearinger, 318; Foster Wild Rice, "Nathaniel Jocelyn, 1796–1881," *Connecticut Historical Society Bulletin* (October 1966), 97–107.

28. See *A Retrospective Exhibition of the Work of Frederick R. Spencer, 1806–1875* (Utica, New York: Munson-Williams-Proctor Institute, 1969). The portrait is listed there. It is now under (dirty) glass and

has not been cleaned, probably, since before the 1940s when, apparently, it came to the church, and certainly since 1964 when a book on the artist was in preparation by Laurence B. Goodrich, who died before it could be published. His papers at the Archives of American Art (AAA) contain a description of the painting written in 1967 by a photographer who did his best shooting through dusty glass balanced atop a step ladder. His black-and-white photograph is also in the file of the AAA. The painting is illustrated, with a short description, in Liscomb, "New Era," 12. Until it can be cleaned and moved to a better location, my description must be based on those as well as my own awkward inspection of the work in situ. (My attempts from long range to have the painting conserved have proven futile.)

29. The geometrical diagrams have given rise to much popular esoteric speculation that can be most easily accessed in Burkhard Bilger, "Mystery on Pearl Street," *The New Yorker* (January 7, 2008), and more fully in a blog by Alan B. Solomon at http://home.earthlink.net?-eastfour/index_paper.htm. R. Lance Factor's *Chapel in the Sky: Knox College's Old Main and its Masonic Architect* (DeKalb, IL: Northern Illinois University Press, 2010), carries it into the land of fantasy.

30. Since I have not been able to see the medal clearly due to the present condition and position of the painting, I cannot confirm the identification of St. George and the dragon on it. Its prominence in the image certainly suggests that Town was proud of it. Thinking it might have come from the RIBA, I consulted Peter Preston-Morley, a medals expert in London, but he assures me that, if it is St. George, it is not a medal from that institution.

31. It is easily assumed that Thomas Cole's famous painting of *The Architect's Dream* of 1840, a work commissioned by Town and now at the Toledo Museum of Art, is a portrait of Town. It shows a figure perched on a column high above a lake flanked by ancient and medieval monuments. Town did not like the finished product (he wanted a pure landscape). Although hardly a portrait in the usual sense, the figure lounges in a nest of enormous tomes, volumes, and portfolios, the products of the study of the buildings in the distance. The secondary status of draftsmanship is perhaps suggested by a triangle, rule, and dividers almost hidden among the books. Town's erstwhile assistant, James Gallier, reported that he was "no draftsman"; see *Autobiography of James Gallier Architect* (New York: 1864 [reprint Da Capo Press, 1973]), 19.

32. Liscomb, "New Era," 12.

33. See Frederic C. Detwiller, "Thomas Dawes: Boston's Patriot Architect," *Old-Time New England* LXVIII (Summer–Fall, 1977), 1–18, with a reproduction of the painting.

34. Detwiller, "Dawes," 2.

35. Information from Historic New England. Inscribed on the reverse: "Portrait of/Mr. Edwin Pierce/Painted by/R.B. Smith/1840." For Smith (1801–55), see Arthur and Sybil Kern, "Painted by Royal B. Smith," *The Clarion* (Spring 1998), 48–53. The Pierce portrait is not listed there.

36. Hilary Anderson, "Aaron Morse, New Hampshire Architect," *Old-Time New England* 78 (Spring–Summer 2000), 24–40. Ammi B. Young (1800–74), one of the major architects of the Greek Revival in this country, designer of the State House in Montpelier, Vermont (1834–41), and first Architect of the U. S. Treasury, advertised in the *New-Hampshire Patriot and State Gazette* in 1830 the opening of an "Architectural and Drawing School," in Lebanon, and that he executed "Architectural Drawings and Models of all kinds." There is a painted portrait of Young; a bust by James Bogle (ca. 1817–73) dated 1858, at the General Services Administration in Washington, DC, according to Daniel Robbins, *The Vermont State House* (1980), 28; and another said to be of him from the 1840s by one C. Rogers at the Vermont Historical Society. Wikipedia uses the latter in its entry on Young. This shows a man seated, profile left, holding what looks like a mirror or, more likely, a framed slate used in primary classrooms of the period. I doubt that this is the portrait of any architect, although it may show a local school teacher. The Vermont Historical Society has no firm data about artist or sitter.

37. James F. O'Gorman, *Henry Austin* (Middletown, CT: Wesleyan University Press, 2008), chapter 1.

38. An instructive comparison to the Morse image of a newly minted architect is a contemporary portrait (1848) of an unidentified housewright in the Nina Fletcher Little Collection at Historic New England. The sitter holds a large wooden plane, while through a window one sees a finished Federal style house, perhaps his latest work. No books or drawing instruments are in evidence. See Janet Dwyer, *Portraits and Landscapes of Alfred J. Wiggin (1823–1883)* (Gloucester, Mass.: Cape Ann Historical Association, 1980). A study parallel to this one, of portraits of builders, would prove instructive.

39. Canadian Centre for Architecture, PH 1986.0393; see also PH 1986 0450. Skinner American Furniture and Decorative Arts — Sale 2567B, 30 October 2011, Lot 36; *Maine Antiques Digest* (January 2012) (sold for over $15,000). Lot 106 in the same sale was another architect's portrait. Another is in the Matthew R. Isenberg collection, available online at the Daguerreian Society website. Many others must exist in public and private collections.

40. Agnes Addison Gilchrist, *William Strickland, Architect and Engineer, 1788–1854* (Philadelphia, PA: University of Pennsylvania Press, 1950 [reprint Da Capo Press, 1969]), esp. 133; and idem, "Additions to William Strickland," *Journal of the Society of Architectural Historians* 13 (October 1954), Supplement.

41. Helen A. Cooper and others, *Life, Liberty and the Pursuit of Happiness: American Art from the Yale University Art Gallery* (New Haven, CT: Yale University Press, 2008), 126. There is a lithographic copy of the figure without the background by either Alfred Newsam or Cephas Grier Childs, ca. 1830 (one at the American Antiquarian Society, another at the Archives of American Art [although there called an etching]). Two Thomas Sully portraits of Strickland are listed in the Art Inventories Catalog of the Smithsonian Institution. According to Charles Henry Hart, in *A Register of Portraits by Thomas Sully* (Philadelphia, 1909), one was a "Bust 1820," the other a "Head 1836." At the Tennessee Historical Society there is a late bust portrait by Washington B. Cooper also listed on the Art Inventories Catalog. The Athenaeum of Philadelphia has a daguerreotype portrait, half length, without staffage, said to be of the architect.

42. See Amelia Peck, ed., *Alexander Jackson Davis: American Architect 1803–1892* (New York: Rizzoli, 1992).

43. See Jane B. Davies, "Davis and Downing: Collaborators in the Picturesque," in *Prophet with Honor: The Career of Andrew Jackson Downing, 1815–1852*, eds. George B. Tatum and Elisabeth Blair MacDougall (Philadelphia, PA: The Athenaeum of Philadelphia, 1989), 81–123.

44. See James F. O'Gorman, *Accomplished in All Departments of Art: Hammatt Billings of Boston, 1818–1874* (Amherst, Mass.: University of Massachusetts Press, 1998).

45. Avery Architectural and Fine Arts Library, A.J. Davis Collection, 1940.001.00740. A note on the drawing gives the date as 1858. It is reproduced as the frontispiece to Peck, *Davis*, where it is dated ca.

1845. Also at the Avery is the better known watercolor portrait of about 1852 by George Freeman, Mary Goldbeck's father.

46. Mary Woods, "The First American Architectural Journals: The Profession's Voice," *Journal of the Society of Architectural Historians* 48 (June 1989), 129.

3

Portraits of the Later Nineteenth Century

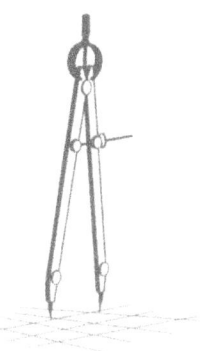

The founding of the American Institute of Architects (AIA) in New York in 1857 created an association of professionals that encouraged the education of its limited membership in artistic and technical matters, the education of the general public in the value of the architect's services (including a respect for his bills), and emphasized the essential role of the architect in the process of building above that of the workman.[1] In the following years, culminating with the founding of *The American Architect and Building News* in Boston in 1876, a series of journals acted as "the profession's voice."[2] With the AIA came, however haltingly at first, an organized lobby for, among other things, the position that, like lawyers or doctors, architects were professionals who provided creative ideas based on a body of knowledge, not merely the act of drawing up buildings. In 1861, for example, Richard Morris Hunt, the AIA's first secretary and third president, took a client to court to gain payment for his design of a New York townhouse, and to establish that he retained ownership of all drawings for the house.[3] Such fees had been at issue since Latrobe's time and continued to be well into the nineteenth century as architects struggled to gain standard recognition of the value of their services, and that drawings were a mere instrument of those services. The transcript of the trial included a succinct and pointed definition by Hunt of the architect as a professional in answer to a question from a court examiner: "You as a lawyer," said Hunt, "when you give your opinion, do not charge for pen, ink and paper, but for your opinion."[4] Hunt was not alone in this: in 1857 Thomas Ustick Walter, the AIA's second president, had said that "Architecture is above all an act of the imagination," whereas Richard Upjohn, the AIA's first president, echoed Walter and Hunt when he told the Institute's annual convention in 1869 that "Our merchandise is our brain, we sell our ideas."[5] That is, the architect, like any other professional, provided intellectual content, the creative product based on learning, not merely the graphic handiwork of a draftsman needed to convey that content. Although the struggle to establish this as fact continued, as did some portraiture incorporating books and drafting instruments, the desire to accent draftsmanship as central to the architect's image waned. Other iconographies began to appear to illuminate the evolving status of the profession.

That status was further enhanced by the establishment after the Civil War of degree-granting schools of architecture at major universities to educate aspiring professionals. The first, at the Massachusetts Institute of Technology in Boston, opened its doors in 1867, to be followed quickly

by others from New York to Illinois and elsewhere. These schools gradually took over the task that had been left to the apprenticeship system of
office-based training since early in the century. Now teachers, many from
abroad (especially Frenchmen educated at the École des Beaux-Arts),
and the libraries and other resources of large educational institutions,
became part of the training for the aspiring designer. And the gradual
introduction of licensing exams by the states ensured that the graduate
architect was thoroughly qualified. The real Latin language degree next
to an officially issued license on the office wall in a sense replaced
depicted instruments and books as testaments of architectural
competence.

THE PERSISTENCE OF TYPE

Nonetheless the old iconography survived in some portraits even beyond
the end of the nineteenth century. There were architects or their artists
who harkened back to pre-1800 precedent. The most cogent example
uncovered during research for this study is the likeness by Lorenzo C.
Scattaglia of Edwin Forrest Durang (1829–1911), a prominent Philadelphia church architect and member of a notable theatrical family, probably
datable to 1874, and now in the collection of the Athenaeum of Philadelphia (Figure 3.1).[6] The artist (b. 1841), a well-known church decorator
in Philadelphia, especially for Roman Catholic congregations, specialized
in "Altar Pieces, Emblematical and Allegorical Figures," and must often
have worked with Durang. In this portrait the bearded, middle-aged
architect sits, formally dressed and rather sad eyed, in a classically paneled
and pilaster-lined interior, his drawing board resting on the kind of
pattered rug seen in much earlier portraits. He proudly displays a book
with paper place-holding tabs, a retractable cloth measuring tape, and
the traditional pair of dividers, which rests points down on a sheet of
paper. Like John Haviland in Neagle's portrait of a half century earlier,
a work either Scattaglia or Durang could easily have known, he seems
emphatically to thrust the dividers toward the viewer. No information is
at hand about the commissioning of this portrait, so the question remains
whether Italian-born Scattaglia or Durang himself consciously sought an
old-fashioned image and knowingly based this work on some traditional
precedent such as the portrait of the Italian Renaissance master, Giacomo
Barozzi da Vignola, taken from the title page of his *Regole delli cinque*

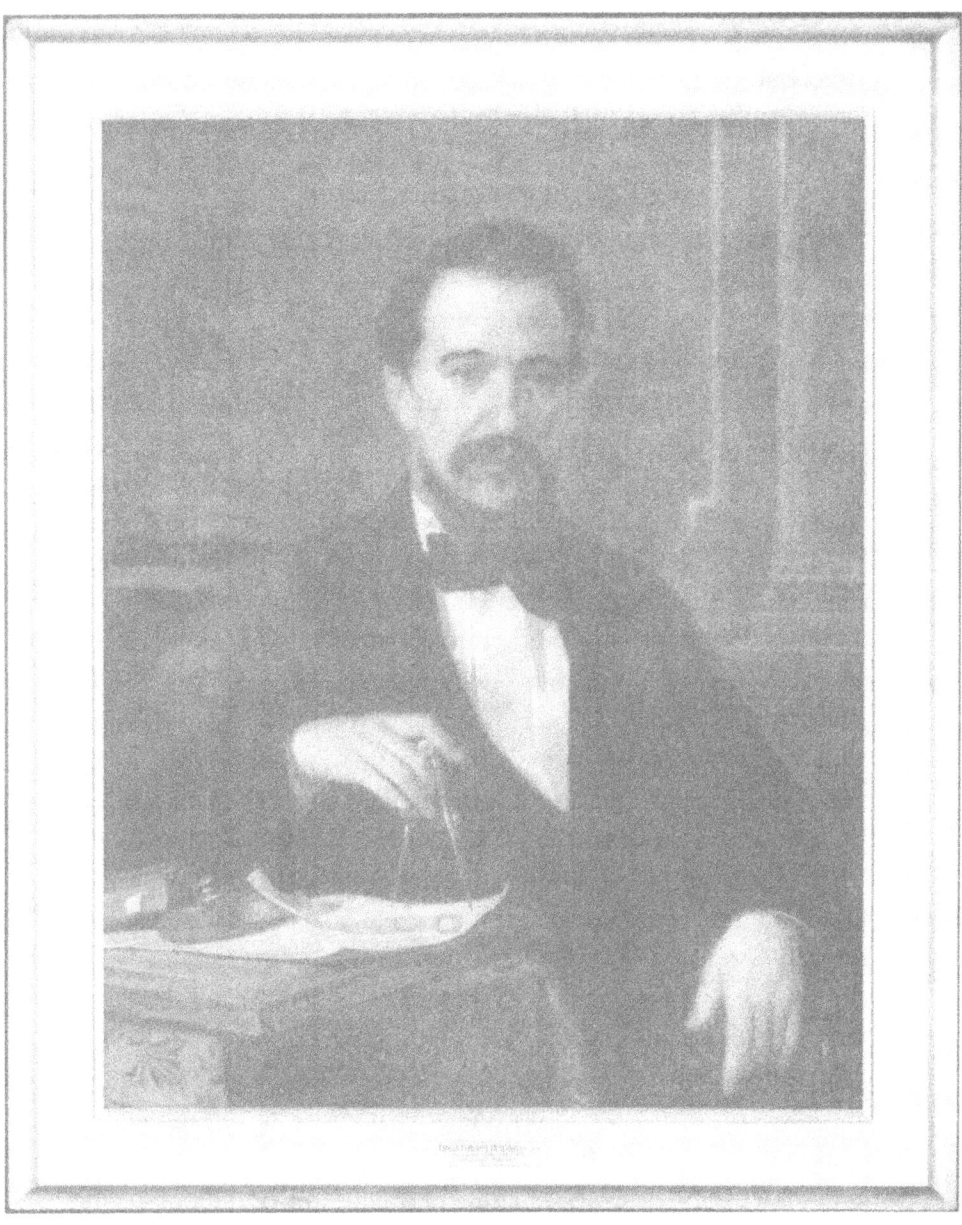

Figure 3.1 Lorenzo C. Scattaglia, *Edwin Forrest Durang*, ca. 1874; 42 x 36 in.
Reproduced courtesy of the Durang Collection, Athenaeum of Philadelphia, Philadelphia, PA.

ordini d'architettura, a book originally published in 1562 (Figure 3.2). Translated and adapted for American usage, it was a staple of the late nineteenth-century design studios and drafting rooms in the period called the American Renaissance. It should also be noted, however, that suggestive precedents closer in time were at hand. Although neither artist nor architect probably knew the original of John Rogers Herbert's 1845 portrait at the Houses of Parliament of well-respected Augustus Welby Northmore Pugin, for example, they might have seen James Henry Lynch's 1853 lithograph copy, and surely knew the much-published neo-Gothic ecclesiastical works of the architect and polemicist.[7] In Herbert's rendering Pugin sits at his table in front of a drawing, with a pair of dividers in his right hand and rule and pencil in his left.

Another version of this continued use of traditionally emblematic dividers is also found in the studio photograph, probably from about 1880, of an unidentified, perhaps New York architect seated in front of a painted backdrop now at the Avery Library, Columbia University.[8] This looks like a publicity image. Our architect poses stiffly at a rug-covered table, of the kind we have seen to be common in daguerreotypes, holding a small pair of dividers as well as either a rule or a scale. Architect or photographer might well have tried in this image to recall earlier daguerreotyped poses. Because this is a staged image, the architect can be holding the dividers only to signify his profession. On the table in front of him are a box of instruments, mechanical pencils, paper, ink bottle, and some small compasses. Propped to one side is the rendering of a Queen Anne house, either his design or one he copied or adapted from some current pattern book. The style of the house and the layout of the sheet, for example, recall Plate 19 of *Modern Architectural Designs and Details* published by William Comstock of New York in 1881.

It is more often possible to say under what conditions a later portrait was created than it is for those created in previous years. Just after the turn of the century, Edwin H. Blashfield produced a portrait of George Browne Post (1837–1913), an engineer trained in architecture by Richard Morris Hunt who would become one of the innovators in the development of the skyscraper in New York City. Although the painting is now at the national headquarters of the AIA in Washington, DC, of which Post had been the sixth president, it was apparently commissioned by the sitter or his family because it was presented to the Institute in 1917, after the architect's death, by the artist and Post's son.[9] Paris-trained Blashfield (1848–1936), best remembered as a muralist who limned the interiors

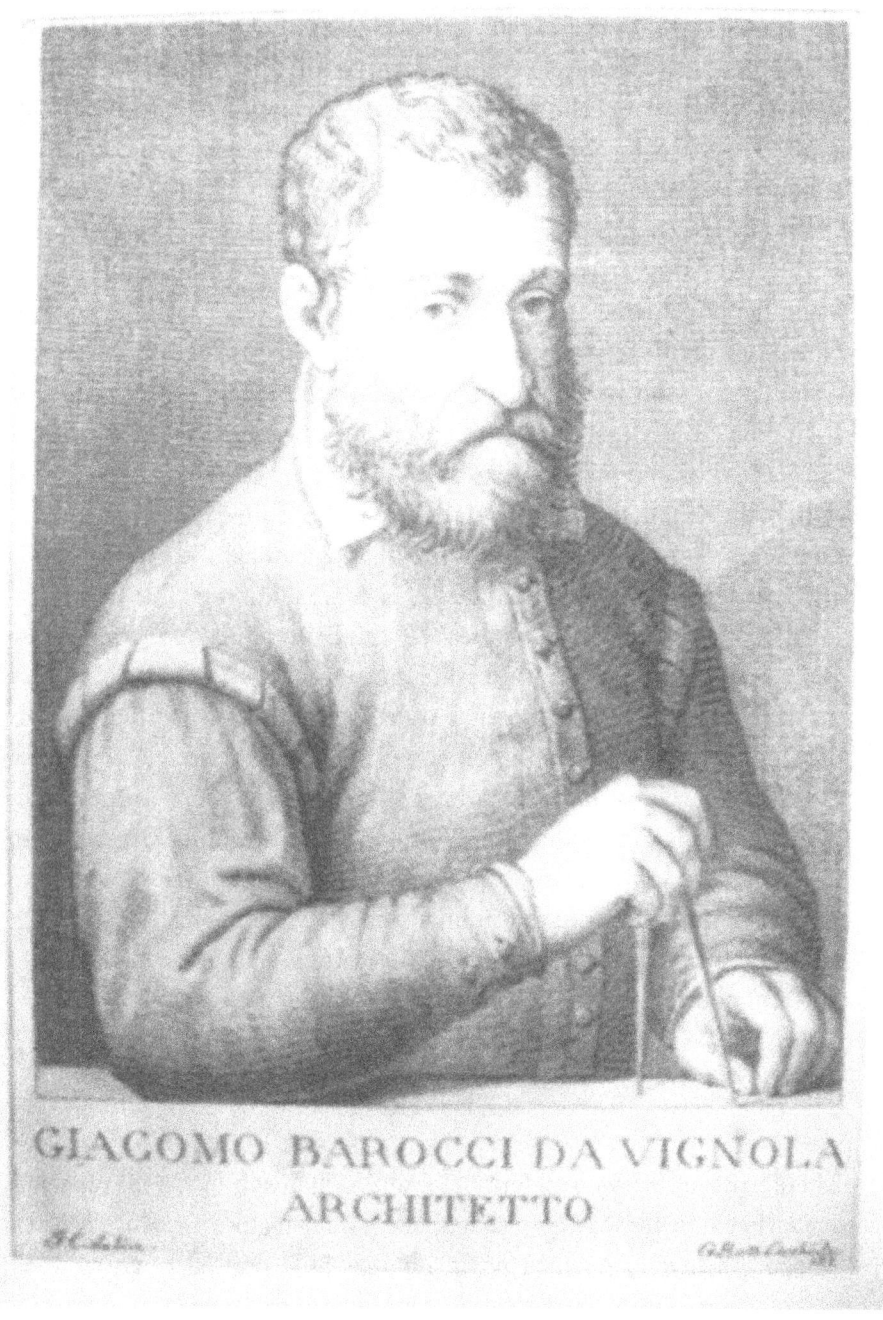

Figure 3.2 Giovanni Battista Cecchi, *Giacomo Barozzi da Vignola*, engraving (from *Regole delli cinque ordini d'architettura*, 1562.

Reproduced courtesy of the Collection Centre Canadien d'Architecture/Canadian Centre for Architecture, Montreal, Canada.

of public buildings by such architects as Post, posed him gazing off into the distance while seated holding a portfolio out of which tumbles a set of blueprints. Iconographically speaking this is the updated version of Buckland's draft and Haviland's rendering. This staging seems to carry a mixed message, for the architect's wandering gaze, so unlike Buckland's confident stare, suggests that he is seeking inspiration, like Ripa's *Theorica*, whereas the blueprints, as reproductions of finished drawings for an established design, represent inspiration congealed. In his right hand is an unidentifiable drawing instrument, perhaps a rule or scale (in another otherwise identical version of this portrait, also by Blashfield, at the National Academy of Design in New York, and probably painted for that institution, it is a pencil[10]), while a pair of dividers here, as in Peale's *Buckland*, lies idle on the table.

Into the twentieth century some architects still enjoyed presenting themselves "on the boards." Boston's Charles Donagh Maginnis (1867–1955) was photographed about 1920 seated at a drafting table in a book-lined room, for example, whereas Charles Allenton Coolidge (1869–1962) of the same city, one of the successors to H. H. Richardson's practice, posed in 1931 with pencil in hand at a drafting board piled with drawings for a painting by Boston portraitist, Charles Sydney Hopkinson (1869–1962) now at the Harvard Art Museums.[11] In such images traditional proclamations of drafting skill survived in dwindling numbers into the twentieth century, especially on the part of architects producing traditional work, but as Jeffery Schnapp has shown, the prevailing iconography in images of cutting-edge modern architects had taken a very different course.[12]

NEW ICONS

There exists an image of Henry Hobson Richardson (1838–86) that fits somewhat into the category that includes Scattaglia's *Durang*. Marian Hooper ("Clover") Adams's posed photographic portrait of about 1884 at the Massachusetts Historical Society shows him seated at a desk in a book-lined room hung with works of art. That room was in the Washington, DC house Clover shared with her husband, Henry. Her gender and her upper-class status precluded showing her photography publically, so this was intended as a private memento; it surely never received a broad viewing until published by modern scholarship.[13] On the desk is a sheet

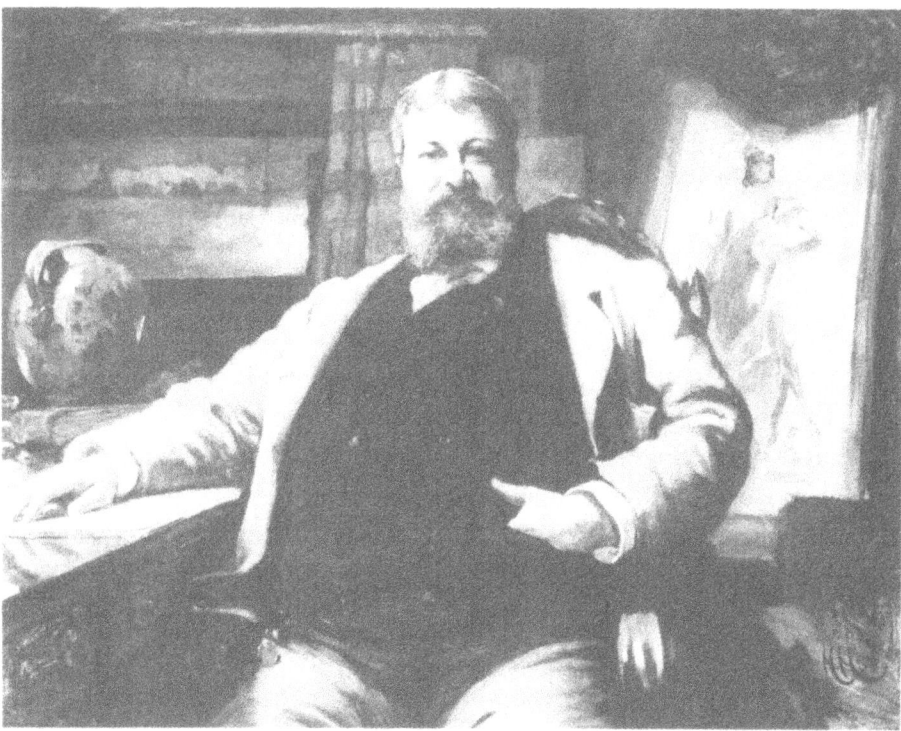

Figure 3.3   Hubert von Herkomer, *Henry Hobson Richardson*, 1885–86; oil on canvas, 44 ¹/2 x 46 ¹/4 in.
Reproduced courtesy of the National Portrait Gallery, Smithsonian Institution, Washington, DC.

of drafting paper and the architect holds against it a shiny straight edge. What might be a wooden case for other instruments rests near his right elbow. Because Richardson was then designing the Adams's Lafayette Square house, as well as the larger adjacent John Hay house on Sixteenth Street, this would seem appropriate, but it is not typical of other images of the man. A different iconographical type that rose after the Civil War is splendidly exemplified by Hubert von Herkomer's portrait of Richardson, painted, like Peale's of Buckland and, as we shall see, John Singer Sargent's of Hunt, at the period of the subject's death, and now in the collection of the National Portrait Gallery in Washington, DC (Figure 3.3). Despite Scattaglia's *Durang*, by this period it was no longer necessary for an architect to suggest his drafting skills. This was especially true of Richardson, the Parisian-trained designer of landmark Trinity Episcopal Church on Copley Square in Boston (1872–77) and other major civic and domestic works, who was perhaps the most celebrated architect in the country by the 1880s. The creator of an eponymous style, the Richardsonian Romanesque, he was also the first American architect to receive a lavishly illustrated monograph focused solely on his work as an architect.[14] Despite Clover Adams's staging, in Richardson's maturity he routinely produced nothing but freehand, thumbnail sketches that were later worked up into architectural drawings by his assistants.[15] Herkomer, soon to become a fashionable British portraitist, had recently taken up oils, and was one of a number of British artists who came to America in the 1880s "to add to their fame and to . . . carry home some of . . . the country's superfluous wealth" according to one contemporary newspaper.[16] Among those Herkomer sought out was Richardson, whose reputation had spread abroad from his studio. The artist produced this likeness in exchange for sketches for his projected house, Lululand, in Bushey, Hertfordshire.[17] Although art takes precedence over professionalism here, this image of the new architect remains important in this study.

A memorable 1885–86 likeness of the human "mountain," as Richardson's friend Phillips Brooks called the rotund architect in his obituary, this portrait, like the other portraits discussed in this and the next paragraph, aims to evoke the character of the sitter. These portraits nonetheless contain sufficient staffage to reveal type. In the painting the architect poses in the brick-built "private study" attached to the wood-framed drafting sheds that extended out from his Brookline, Massachusetts, residence. He sits before the fireplace ingle draped with William Morris fabrics—not, it should be noted, in one of the adjacent drafting stalls called "The Coops." (He was informally photographed in the drafting area, with his back to the camera as he critiqued the work of his assistants, recognizable to historians only because of his black hair, bulk, and baggy coat.) Herkomer impressively staged him beside the huge desk that occupied the center of his library sitting in an Elizabethan-style armchair more often found at his writing desk to the left of the fireplace.[18] Unlike other formally clad sitters discussed here, he is dressed comfortably, even picturesquely, as his staid client John J. Glessner described his later wardrobe, watch fob in evidence, monocle at the ready, directly confronting the viewer with broad body language revealing his ferociously convex midsection. His right hand rests on a blank sheet of writing paper (he often sketched on his stationery); his left tucks into the pocket of his waist coat. He is surrounded by prized objects of international art and *virtù* of the kind that punctuated his study: on the left a currently fashionable *objet d'art*, a blue-and-white porcelain jug sitting on a book, moved for the occasion from the center of the desk, and, resting on an easel on the right, a large framed photograph showing head-on Andrea Verrocchio's equestrian *Barolommeo Colleoni* in the Campo Ss. Giovanni e Paolo in Venice. Richardson had visited the city in the summer of 1882 and acquired several photographs of that statue.[19] What is probably the most famous portrait of a nineteenth-century American architect disappointed a Boston critic when first displayed at the Williams and Everett Gallery. He saw a "vital human being," but searched in vain for a representation of the "genius that has succeeded in creating a new and curiously beautiful architectural style," a chore that would seem difficult for any artist, and a comment off the mark when one considers the visual impact of the portrait itself. The painting remained above the parlor fireplace in the Richardson family home in Brookline until moved to the National Portrait Gallery. A full-size monochromatic heliotype, one of two produced, has hung in the entry hall of Richardson's urban domestic masterpiece, the J. J. Glessner House of 1885–87 in Chicago, almost from the day it was first occupied.[20] In a speech honoring Richardson at Harvard commencement just after his death, Charles Francis Adams, Jr. proposed that the portrait be purchased by the school and hung in Memorial Hall on campus as part of a collection of immortals.[21]

A portrait that is somewhat related iconographically, though it is less dramatic and of a less picturesquely flamboyant man, is that of Daniel Hudson Burnham (1860–1920), painted in 1899 by Sweden's Anders Zorn, now at the United States Commission of Fine Arts in Washington, DC (Figure 3.4). Burnham was the original chairman of that Commission when it was called the Council. The painting stayed in the family until it came to its present location in 1958 as a gift from Burnham's sons. (This portrait is perhaps better known by the copy made just after Burnham's death by Arvid Frederik Nyholm now in the library named for the architect at the Chicago Art Institute.) Burnham, distinguished as head of a large Chicago office and lead architect of the Chicago World's Fair of 1893, became even more famous as a planner of cities from San Francisco to Chicago and Washington, DC.[22] Zorn (1860–1920) was to become an internationally acclaimed artist who focused on portraits of well-known sitters (he painted Grover Cleveland in the year be portrayed Burnham), but is perhaps better known for his outdoor scenes of ravishingly naked females. He, like Herkomer, came to America to extend his reputation, and during the Chicago Fair met Burnham, who later wrote to say he admired his portrait of Augustus Saint-Gaudens. Burnham commissioned this work. "The sort of portraits that stir my blood," he

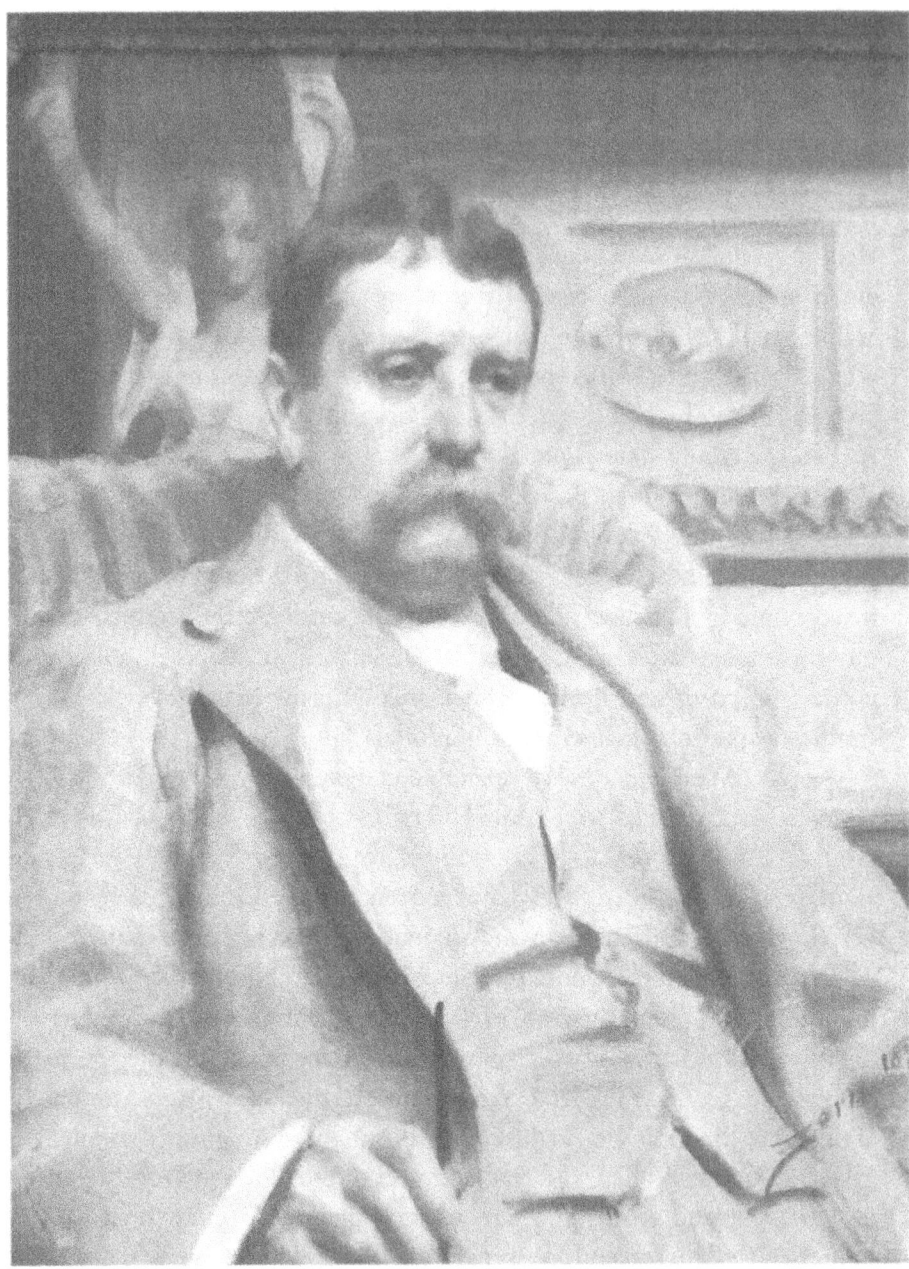

Figure 3.4 Anders Leonard Zorn, *Daniel Hudson Burnham*, 1899; oil on canvas, 30 x 25 in.
Reproduced courtesy of the U. S. Commission of Fine Arts, Washington, DC.

wrote the artist, "are those that are painted boldly under a strong impulse—that are full of mystery. No one but you can do this supreme work." [23] Whether the portrait lives up to this description or not, a description that seems somewhat better fitted to Herkomer's *Richardson*, here too the architect is not shown at a drafting board, although he does hold a pencil or pen in his right hand. He wears a suit and sits comfortably, if pensively perhaps, at a writing desk in the library of his home in Evanston, Illinois, where the picture was painted—not at his architectural office. He is in front of an ornamental fireplace frame made for the Fair. Vintage photographs show that the finished portrait hung above this domestic fireplace on whose mantel shelf rested objects of art and *virtù*, including a cast of the hooded head of Augustus Saint-Gaudens's Adams Memorial in Rock Creek Cemetery in Washington, DC. These do not appear in the portrait, but a part of one of the classical caryatid figures with uplifted arms flanking the fireplace opening, and an oval relief panel from the frame at Burnham's back, suggest the cultured ambience in which he lived and worked.

The same is true of a portrait, perhaps posthumous, of Richard Upjohn (1802–78), yet another English immigrant who became a founder and, as mentioned previously, the first president of the AIA as well as, in his time, the most influential architect of churches in the country. [24] Although research has thus far found no documentation for this commission, and the comments below are based solely on a colored half-tone copy in the Prints and Photographs Division of the Library of Congress, it seems related to a posthumous bust portrait dated 1899, painted in profile by Anna Milo Upjohn (1868–1951), at the AIA headquarters in Washington, DC. The version in the half-tone shows Upjohn in profile, a pose rare in architects' portraits of the period and unique in this study, seated before a glass-fronted, diamond-paned bookcase on which rests a small unidentified statuette. [25] The upper left corner is occupied by the curved fragment of a framed painting. What these three otherwise different portraits have in common, portraits showing the sitter outside the drafting room and without drafting tools but surrounded by *objets d'art*, is the projection of the architect as a cultured gentleman. [26] And they do it even when, like Burnham, the architect was also a corporate giant, one who as a young man said his "idea is to work up a big business ... deal with big businessmen, and build up a big organization," and by the time the portraitist had captured him, he had accomplished just that. [27]

When these portraits were painted these men were established professional architects, and the portraits convey an image that is a far cry from
that of the emerging architects of earlier in the century. In fact, such
paintings also stand somewhat outside the type of likenesses of many other
late nineteenth-century architects, Richardson's more than Burnham's or
Upjohn's. The series of studio photographs taken of Richardson in the
early 1880s by George Collins Cox (1851–1903), famed among other
things for his portraits of Walt Whitman, reconfirm that this architect
was not your typical professional. They show him standing or seated at
a carpeted table dressed in a medieval monk's costume with books and
beer mug as staffage, the dress and ambience a visual proclamation of
his inspiration from medieval architecture, influenced in part by A. W.
N. Pugin and William Morris, which led to his personal interpretation
of the Romanesque style.[28] (One wonders to what extent these staged
photographs owe something to the frontispiece of Pugin's *True Principals
of Pointed or Christian Architecture* [1841], which depicts a monk-archi-
tect seated at his work.) In Brookline Richardson ran a suburban atelier
not an urban office. The total number of his executed buildings was
small compared to other major architects of the period. He was prodigal
with money, dying early and deeply in debt. Burnham's career as head
of a large firm in Chicago was more in keeping with the age in which the
successful urban professional architect, and the business of architecture,
reached full flower. Most men who ran the corporate firms becoming
common in this period, large firms turning out series of skyscrapers and
other complex, structurally innovative, monumental, or big-budget public
or commercial buildings, would not want to be shown as picturesquely
as Herkomer showed Richardson, or with drawing tools, as Scattaglia
showed Durang, any more than they would want to be shown holding
the hammer and saw of a carpenter or the trowel of a mason. Rules
and dividers were now properly placed in the hands of assistants, the
indistinguishable "line-makers," as one observer called them, out in the
drafting pool.[29] It was a matter of class. Such a principal, his name on
the door, would want to be pictured to himself as well as to others, as a
man of affairs, a leader in the world of business on a status akin to that
of his clients, and socially and professionally well above that of his help.[30]
Draftsmen were not admitted to the AIA until 1900, and then only with
nearly prohibitive qualifications.[31]
    Increasingly after the Civil War, photography vied with the painted
portrait. What can be assumed to be a publicity photograph, now at the

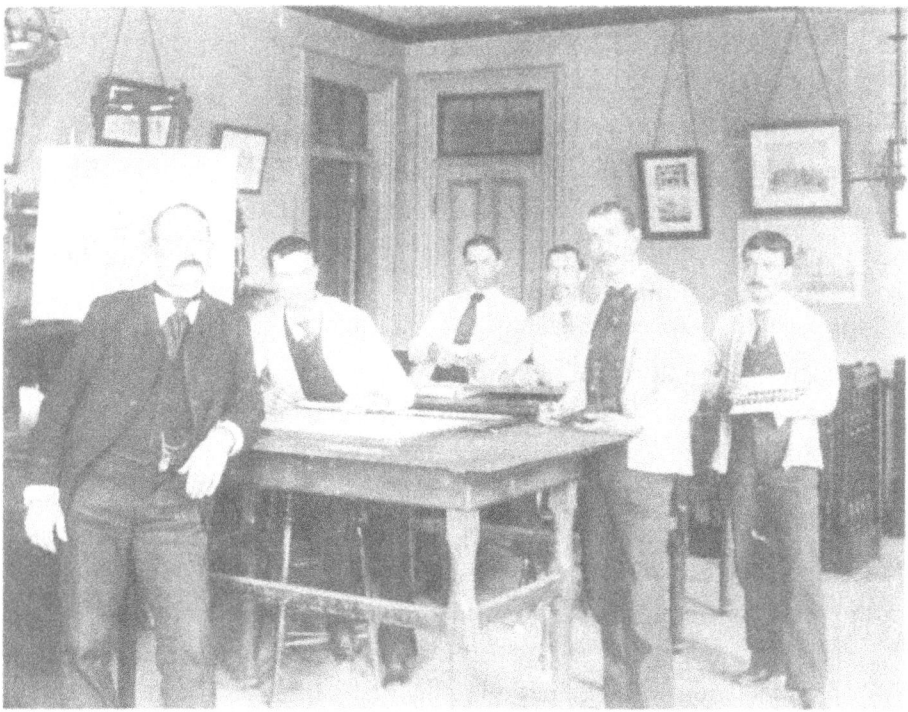

Figure 3.5 Unknown photographer, *The Office of George M. Coombs*, 1894.
Reproduced courtesy of the Maine Historic Preservation Commission, Augusta, ME.

Maine Historic Preservation Commission in Augusta, of the office of
George M. Coombs in Lewiston, taken in 1894, illustrates the gulf
between the principal and his draftsmen (Figure 3.5). Coombs (1851–
1909) was a major Maine architect of the last third of the nineteenth
century, and the founder of a busy firm that exists to this day as Harriman
Associates. Rather than in the drafting room, as here, he would have
worked out of a private office. The photograph clearly distinguishes the
principal in the left foreground who is dressed in a business suit and tie,
with a gold watch chain hanging from a vest button, and who prominently
displays two idle hands, clean and empty, unencumbered by drafting
instruments, unstained by India ink. Behind him stand identically jack-
eted, interchangeable draftsmen — the drafting pool — holding for display
the traditional signs of their trade — T-square, triangles, ruling pens, and
one, the man on the right, the office perspectivist or renderer, with his
set of watercolor pigments. On the walls are displayed drawings illustrating
the products of Coombs's brain as made visible at the hands of his

instrument-wielding line-makers.[32] The uniform dress of the employees we see here may not have been general in the drafting rooms, but that Combs's firm does not represent an isolated example of such discrimination is more subtly suggested by a posed publicity photograph at the Minnesota Historical Society of the staff of Cass Gilbert's office taken about 1900. The image includes a drafting table, T-square and triangle, a plan of the architect's Minnesota State Capitol of 1895, and the line-makers (one flaunting another T-square). Although all are dressed in suits, only Gilbert (1858–1934), seated in the center, shows his hands through a gap in the line of drafting tables, and those hands are empty.[33] In Kenyon Cox's half-length portrait of 1907 in the collection of the National Academy of Design, a seated Gilbert appears as a turn-of-the-century plutocrat, flashing stick pin, fat cigar, and all.[34] Where once showing one's drafting instruments separated architect from builder, it seems that now their absence in most portraits of the period distinguished the principal from his underlings as a member of his clients' class.[35]

How else might such principals be portrayed? There was one type of representation in architects' portraits that carried over from earlier. Although drafting instruments represented handwork, books demonstrated an individual's intellectual preparation. If displays of drawing tools thin out after mid-century in architects' portraits as they gained assurance of a professional status akin to that of a lawyer, doctor, or banker, books continued to represent acquired knowledge or cultural status, especially in the period of academic historicism in architectural design that was the late nineteenth and early twentieth century. And the single book or small stack of books of earlier images now often gives way to representations of large collections. The pioneering Boston pictorialist, F. Holland Day (1864–1933), sometime around 1900 photographed his friend and associate Bertram Grosvenor Goodhue (1869–1924), erstwhile partner of Ralph Adams Cram, renowned architect of the Nebraska State Capitol (1924) and other works, and draftsman and graphic designer of great distinction.[36] He is seated in a shallow space, head resting on arm resting on books resting on a table. His likeness is backed edge to edge by shelves of more books. The print is in the Clarence H. White Collection in the Division of Prints and Photographs at the Library of Congress. Although it might be supposed that a Day photograph of Goodhue would be considered more a work of art or a personal memento than a professional portrait, the same cannot be said of a similar although half-length image of Henry Hornbostel (1867–1961) of about 1910. Over a long career in

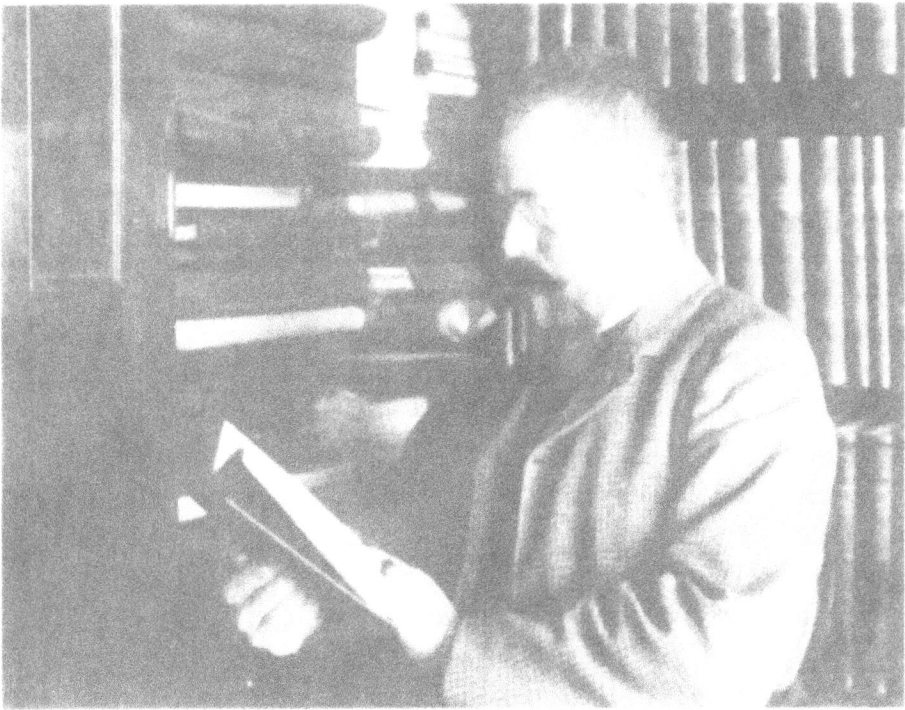

Figure 3.6 Unknown photographer, *John Calvin Stevens*, ca. 1900.
Reproduced courtesy of the Maine Historic Preservation Commission, Augusta, ME.

New York and Pittsburgh, Hornbostel proved to be an innovative classicist responsible for well over 200 buildings, most of them important ones. In this photograph he stands at a table looking at folios and drawings of architecture, while the background is filled with cased shelves of other books. Surely this image was for public consumption.[37] Another photographer, about 1900, posed Maine's most famous architect, gifted draftsman, and artist, John Calvin Stevens (1855–1940), in the middle of his long career engrossed in one volume and surrounded by groaning shelves of others, presumably in the library of his office.[38] In this publicity image, now housed in the Stevens Collection at the Maine Historical Society in Portland, he could be a lawyer researching a case, a professional association he would presumably have welcomed (Figure 3.6). But not all such portraits flaunted large book collections. There is the well-known posed photograph of about 1890 at the Ryerson and Burnham Library of the Art Institute of Chicago showing Daniel Burnham and his partner, John Wellborn Root (1850–91), seated facing each other in what looks to be the library of their office in The Rookery, one of their early Chicago skyscrapers. This too must have been intended for public consumption. Burnham holds a book while others are casually stacked on the floor at his feet. Root grasps drawings while a portfolio rests against the leg of his chair. No drafting tools are in evidence, but a statue of divine Venus reigns overhead as their cultural icon and guiding deity.[39]

The change in the representation of the architect that occurred after mid-century can be succinctly demonstrated by comparing two portraits of Thomas Ustick Walter (1804–87). In a studio photograph taken after Walter had become the famed designer of the dome and wings of the federal Capitol in the 1850s, he presents himself as any other professional or man of affairs. He is seated, dressed in a business suit, and displays no signs of any "trade" (Figure 3.7)[40] That this was an updated image of a man who as a youth apprenticed as a mason can be made clear if we glance back some twenty years to a lithograph by Albert Newsam after an 1835 portrait of Walter by John Neagle (both now at the Athenaeum of Philadelphia) commissioned by the architect for his family, in which the newly minted designer proudly holds a draftsman's scale while resting his left elbow on a book (Figure 3.8). The scale was shown as an alternative to dividers or other instruments as a sign of his elevation to the status of draftsman. In the original oil (which lost the essential details just mentioned in a later alteration) a view of Walter's Moyamensing Prison of 1831–35 peeks out from behind the base of a column in the background.[41]

Formal painted or photographed portraits of architects in the guise of businessmen, such as that just mentioned of T. U. Walter, which focus on individual likeness and not on the sitter's specific occupation, became characteristic in the second half of the nineteenth century and continued into the next. Representative is William De Leftwich Dodge's portrait of John Merven Carrère (1858–1911) of about 1905 in the collection of the National Portrait Gallery (Figure 3.9). It was based on a photograph by Dodge (1867–1935), who shows Carrère, a principal in Carrère and Hastings, one of the outstanding Beaux-Arts firms in the country, seated dressed in a business suit, his hands folded in his lap. There is no staffage. As Mary Woods observed, Carrère's office, like those of many of his peers, "emulated the specialization and bureaucratization of American business conglomerates."[42] As we have seen, there had always been portraits of American architects lacking instruments and/or books, but images such as these, of leading professional architects depicted as members of the

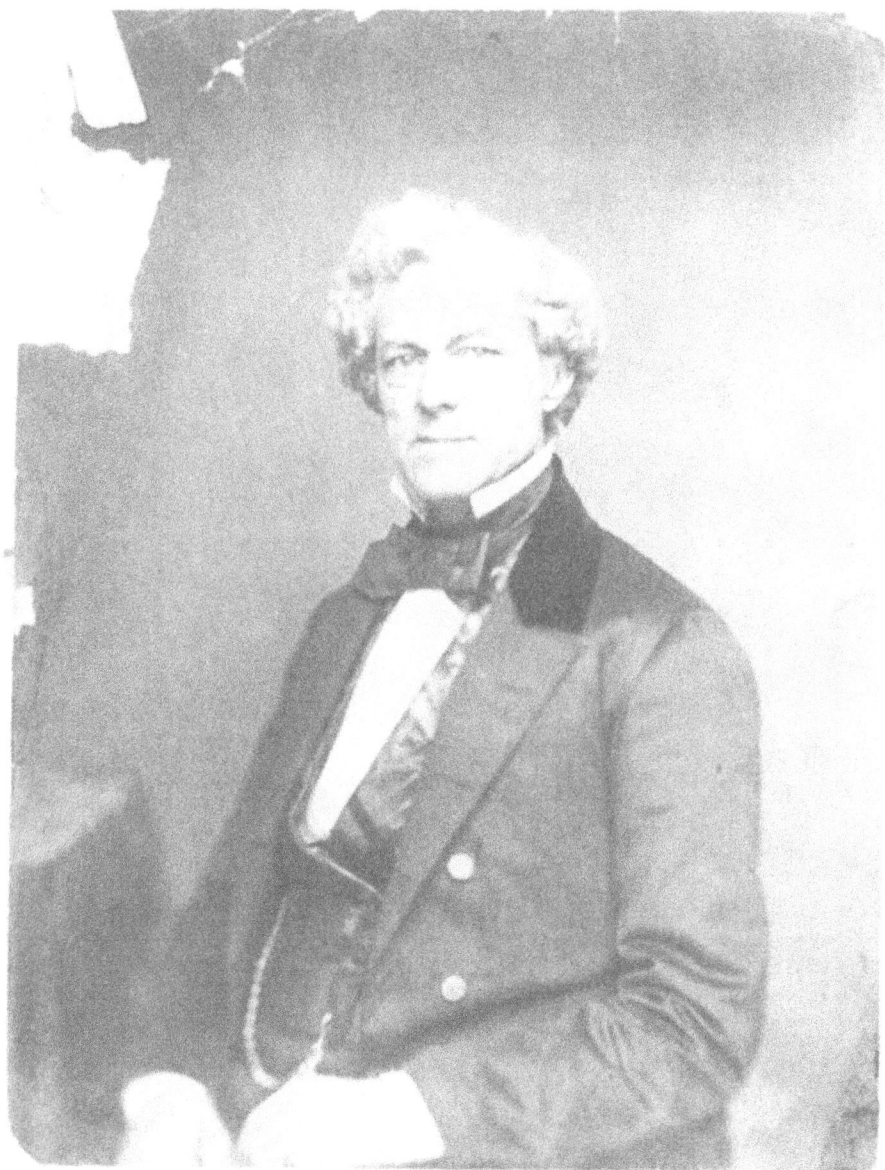

Figure 3.7 Unknown photographer, *Thomas Ustick Walter*, ca. 1853.
Reproduced courtesy of the Athenaeum of Philadelphia, Philadelphia, PA.

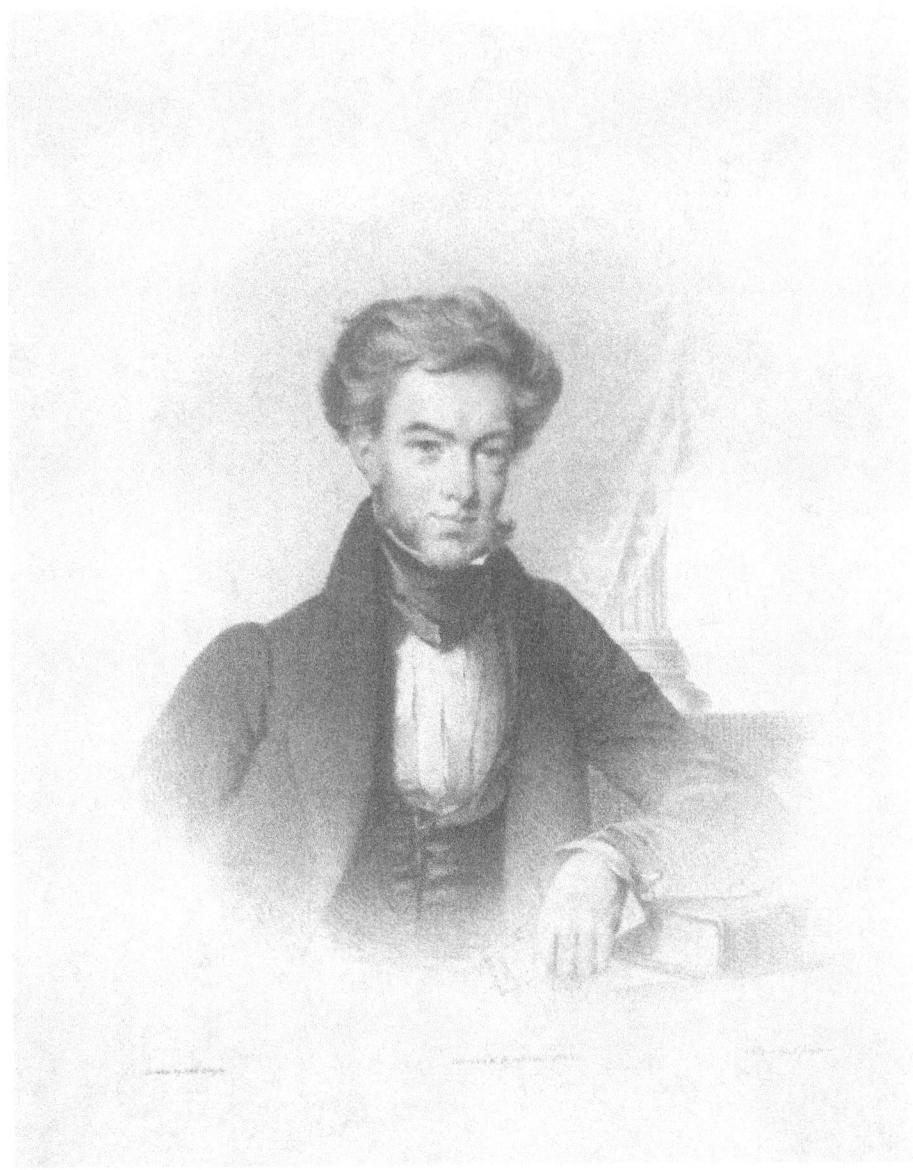

Figure 3.8 Alfred Newsam after John Neagle, *Thomas Ustick Walter*, 1836.
Reproduced courtesy of the Athenaeum of Philadelphia, Philadelphia, PA.

managerial class, became even more common after the Civil War, and must be seen in historical context. A seated John Carrère looks out at us as does a seated William Buckland, but the difference in meaning is marked between the two images by the presence or absence of the tools of their métier.

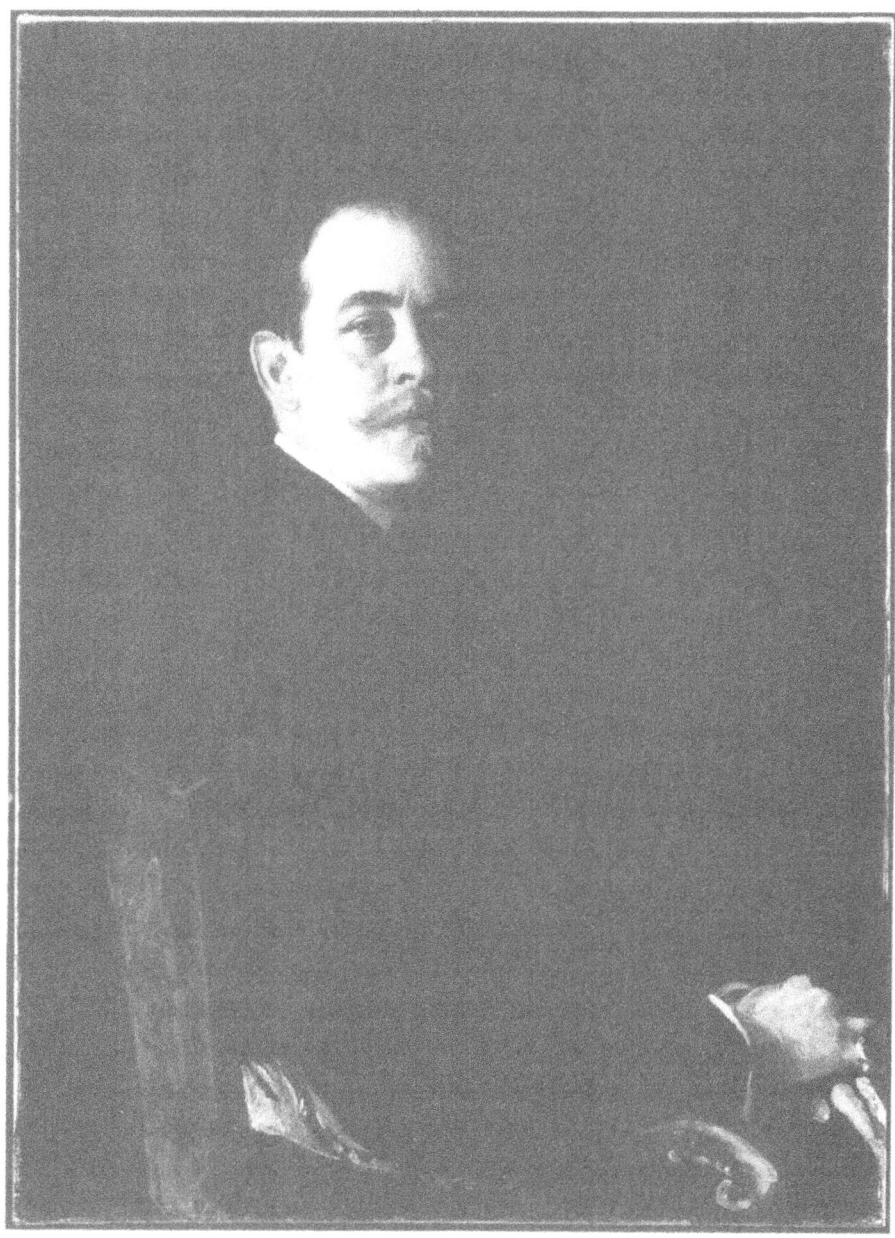

Figure 3.9 William de Leftwich Dodge, *John Merven Carrère*, ca. 1905; oil on canvas, 40 ³/16 x 30 in.

Reproduced courtesy of the National Portrait Gallery, Smithsonian Institution, Washington, DC.

That such painted portraits existed in numbers around 1900 is perhaps well illustrated by the series of sober likenesses commissioned for a "Hall of Fame" established by the Chicago Chapter of the AIA in 1913.[43] These represented the leading architects who collectively rebuilt Chicago after the fire of 1871 and led in the creation of the modern urban environment through the development of the tall, steel-framed office building. Their portraits are now in the Chicago History Museum but were originally displayed in the Chapter's room at the Art Institute, a context in which the stature of the sitters in the profession was understood. There were eventually eighteen portraits of men such as Peter B. Wight, William LeBaron Jenney, Daniel Burnham, Solon Spencer Beman, Dankmar Adler, Louis Sullivan, and so on. Adler (1844–1900), Sullivan's erstwhile and indispensible partner, appears in a posthumous image painted by Oskar Gross in 1916. Viennese-trained Gross (1872–1963) emigrated from Hungary at the behest of Daniel Burnham and landed in Chicago as a mural painter, but by 1911 he had switched to portraiture. Adler is seated, silhouetted against a neutral background, legs crossed, fingers entwined over his stomach. It is an image of satisfied contentment, and probably based on a photograph. Wight (1838–1925), a pioneer in fire-resistant commercial construction, is represented in 1913 by another local portraitist, Paris-trained Allen Erskine Philbrick (1879–1964). He too sits isolated within the frame, sad-eyed, holding an unidentifiable book in his left hand, a finger of which marks the place at which his reading has been interrupted. Oskar Gross's 1916 portrait of less-remembered Frederick Baumann (1826–1921) depicts him empty handed. The 1916 portrait of Burnham by Oliver Dennett Grover (1861–1927), a student of Duveneck and Whistler who taught at the Art Institute, shows staffage but that is minimal. On the desk at which the architect sits are some books and paper, the latter more letter than drawing size. As this and other Burnham portraits show, he was a man who worked seated at a desk like a businessman, not a drafting table. Many other paintings in the series are mere head and shoulder likenesses, like Jenney's (1832–1907) of 1914, also posthumous. With such images, these professional architects were elevated into the realm of the iconic, although they now linger, largely unremarked, in museum storage.[44] *Sic transit gloria mundi.*

How else could such men be portrayed? As we have seen, many architects were depicted half length and seated, but some notable photographs and especially painted likenesses now took on the more traditional iconographical pose of aristocratic, seemingly larger-than-life figures.

They are often shown three-quarter or full-length, and the result varies somewhat. A photograph of Dankmar Adler of about 1880 at the Burnham Library of the Art Institute of Chicago anticipates this. It shows him suited, full length, standing amid generic studio props, legs crossed, leaning on a draped support, left arm akimbo. It was probably more a personal than a professional image, but it stands in marked contrast to that of the Avery Library's photograph from the same time that we have discussed previously, of an unidentified New York architect posed in a studio at a drafting table. Thomas Eakins's unfinished, 1896, life-size painting of university-trained John Joseph ("Dickey") Borie III (1869–1926), a work entitled simply *The Architect*, and now in the collection of the Hood Art Museum at Dartmouth College, is a special representative of this type. One assumes it was commissioned by Borie himself or his family; it remained with relatives until it entered the collection at Dartmouth. The work may be heroic in size and format but one wonders whether the subject deserved the honor. This is one case in which the visual distinction between draftsman and principal was not followed. Philadelphia's best-known artist shows a twenty-seven-year-old local aristocrat who trained as an architect, drafted in the Philadelphia office of Cope and Stewardson for a few years, and beginning in 1899, after posing for Eakins, designed Allerton House near Monticello, Illinois, for a friend, a manor inspired by a seventeenth-century English prototype. By 1905 he had moved permanently to England where he worked as an interior designer. The sitter—or rather, stander—is not drawing at, but nonchalantly leaning on, an upturned—hence idle—tilt-top drafting table. Eakins left a diagram demonstrating how he enhanced Borie's height in the picture, but, despite its size and Eakins's manipulation, this is less a heroic figure than the portrait of a typical Main Line dandy.[45]

Frank A. Werner's three-quarter length, life-size portrait of still much-revered Louis Sullivan (1856–1924) at the Chicago History Museum, also among the portraits in the local chapter of the AIA's Hall of Fame, is more impressive. It shows Adler's partner, Frank Lloyd Wright's *Lieber Meister*, and perhaps the most passionate architect and most gifted decorative draftsman ever produced in this country, in a commanding pose turned slightly toward the viewer, with one arm akimbo, the other resting on what might be a blank sheet of drawing paper, and the interrupted gleaming lines of his watch chain pointing toward his hands. His gaze avoids the viewer (Figure 3.10). Werner (1877–1955) was a noted Chicago portrait painter educated in Germany and in engineering at MIT.[46] The

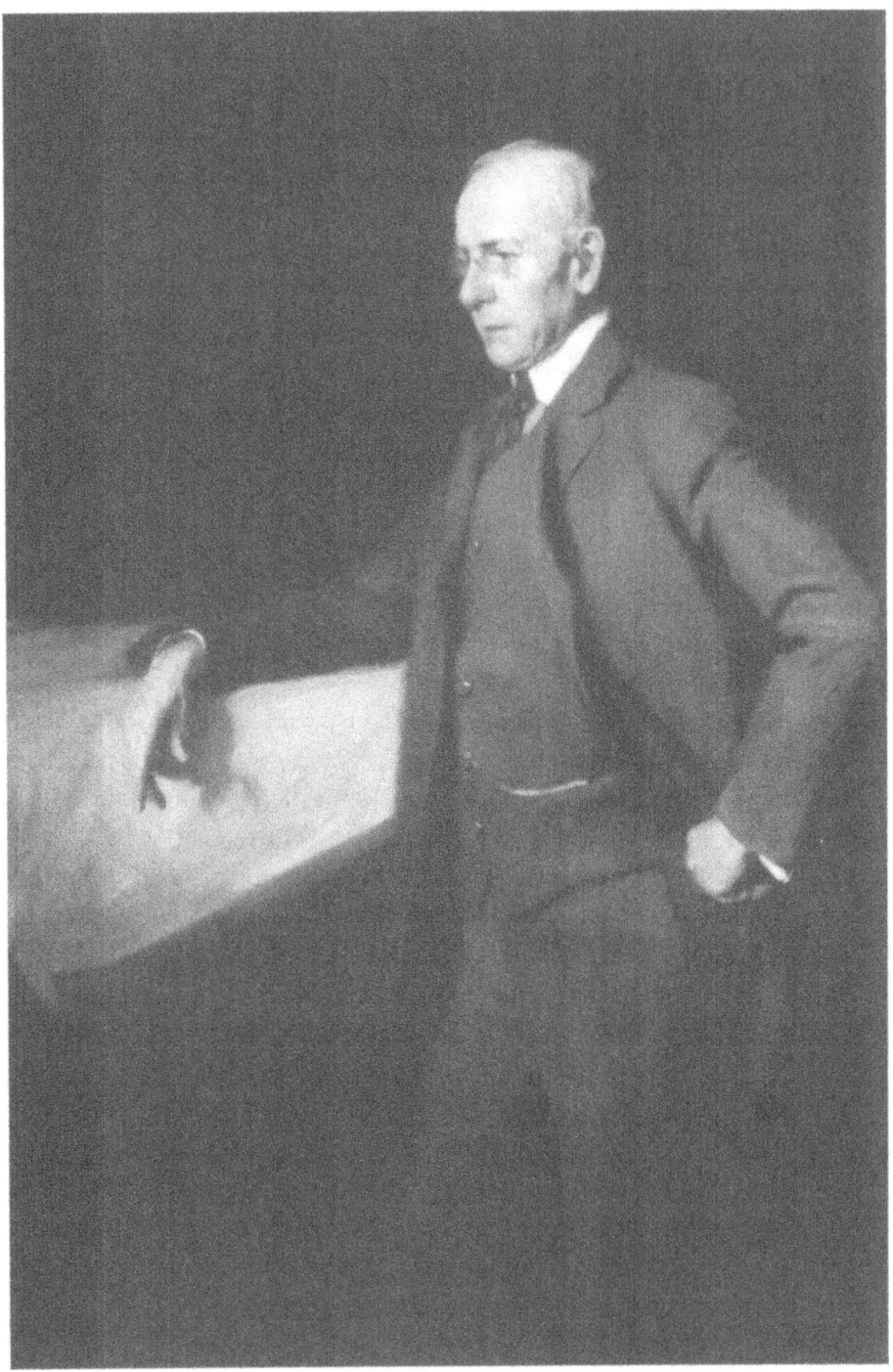

Figure 3.10 Frank A. Werner, *Louis H. Sullivan*, 1919; oil on canvas, 63 $^1/_2$ x 41 $^1/_2$ in.
Reproduced courtesy of the Chicago History Museum, Chicago, IL.

painting won the coveted Logan Medal with its purse of $500 at the annual exhibition of Chicago artists held at the Art Institute at the beginning of 1919. It was published in a review of the show in the *Fine Arts Journal*, where it was described tersely as "low-toned, dignified and a true likeness," but savaged by the critic for the *Chicago Tribune*, who hinted that the prize was awarded for other than artistic merit. That critic may have been referring to the fact that Werner was a member of the Chicago Commission for the Encouragement of Local Art chaired by Frank G. Logan, who with his wife donated the prize. Logan and Werner gave the portrait to the Hall of Fame in 1926.[47] It was painted at the lowest period in Sullivan's career, yet the artist makes him look like a man in charge, a corporate manager or, better perhaps, a preacher (which, in a way, he was).[48]

The capstone of this late-century development, the ultimate rendering of the architect as a person who stands on his own commanding recognition, unaided by props other than the ambience in which he stands, is John Singer Sargent's portrait of Parisian-trained Richard Morris Hunt (1827–95), painted—like those of Buckland and Richardson—near the time of his death (Figure 3.11).[49] The work is appropriately owned by Biltmore House, Hunt's 255-room, dream-of-history mansion on 125,000 acres for George Washington Vanderbilt at Asheville, North Carolina, for which it was commissioned. There it has been since finished, displayed in an ornate gilt frame *nine feet tall*, facing from its original position across the Salon toward Sargent's companion portrait of landscape architect Frederick Law Olmsted.[50] Hunt was known as a brilliant draftsman, a man who once advised his students to "Draw, draw, draw! Sketch, sketch, sketch! . . . [I]t will . . . give you a certain control of your pencil so that you can the more rapidly express on paper your thoughts in designing." But that was earlier in his career. As we have seen, in the New York court case mentioned previously, he had elevated conception over drawing as the true work of the architect, and he had become the principal in a large firm. As Mary Woods wrote, in a statement that succinctly captures the thrust of the second half of this discourse, his "move from a studio [in 1858] to office building . . . reveals his evolution from cultivated artist-architect to a tough-minded businessman."[51]

In Sargent's painting Hunt is no draftsman. There is in English art an old formula for aristocratic portraiture that posed milord in front of his country house, and Sargent (1856–1925), a most distinguished portrait painter of international reputation, has followed it here even though

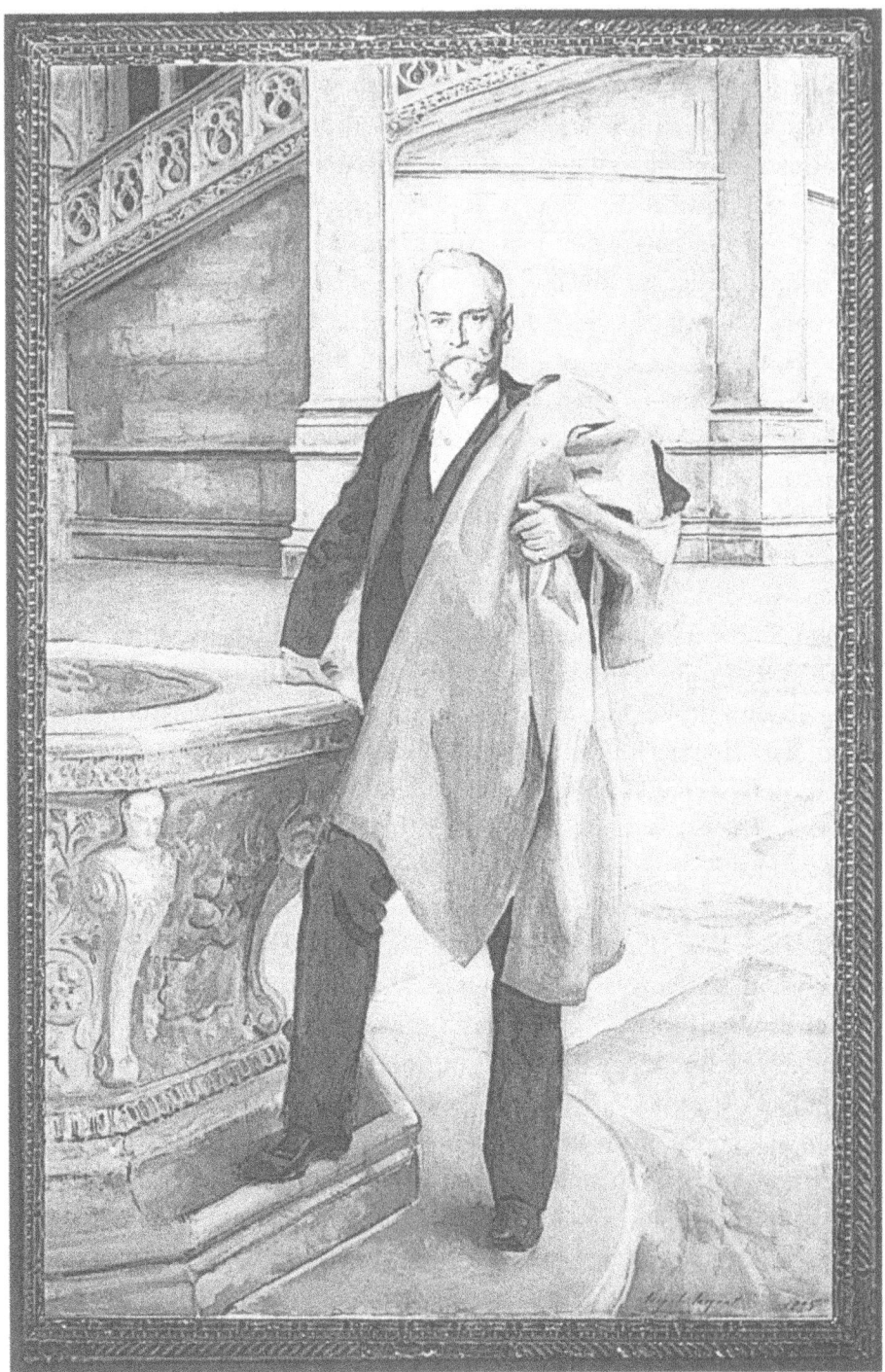

Figure 3.11 John Singer Sargent, *Richard Morris Hunt,* 1895; oil on canvas, 90 ³/4 x 59 ³/4 in.

Reproduced with permission from The Biltmore Company, Ashville, NC.

Hunt was the designer of Biltmore, not its owner. Posing in front of the chateau, the architect projects the air, the nonchalance, of an aristocrat, and more. Given the way Sargent has shown him with his overcoat thrown toga-like over his left shoulder, we could, if we would, read him as a Roman emperor. He stands at ease next to the ornamental well head and in front of the external *François-Premier* staircase of Vanderbilt's great house. He is far from an architectural office. There is no suggestion of his profession. He might be the owner rather than the creator of the establishment, but to one who knows him to have been the architect, he seems to have willed it into existence by the force of his genius. He strikes us now as the antecedent of the modern "starchitect." (It might be useful to recall that Hunt is also honored in a monumental neo-classical exedra on the Central Park side of Fifth Avenue between 70th and 71st streets in New York dedicated in 1900, a public memorial that contains a portrait bust by Daniel Chester French flanked by allegorical representations of Art and Architecture. There is nothing else like it in this country.[52]) In such a portrait as that at Biltmore House the architect is pictured not only professionally established but socially at the level of any client. He could be a member of a late nineteenth- or early twentieth-century commercial, professional, or idle class, one of the kind of men we now refer to as "suits."[53]

NOTES

1. See Henry H. Saylor, *The A.I.A.'s First Hundred Years* (Washington, DC: The Octagon, 1957).

2. Mary Woods, "The First American Architectural Journals: The Profession's Voice," *Journal of the Society of Architectural Historians* 48 (June 1989), 117–138.

3. Paul R. Baker, *Richard Morris Hunt* (Cambridge, Mass., M.I.T. Press, 1980), 80–87.

4. Hunt vs. Parmly, Superior Court, New York, as reported in *Architects and Mechanics Journal* III (February 1861), 233. See also Saylor, *The A. I. A.'s First Hundred Days*, 53–57.

5. Woods, "The First American Architectural Journals," 124; and Mary N. Woods, *From Craft to Profession* (Berkeley, CA: University of California Press, 1999), 19.

6. See "Philadelphia Architects and Building" online at http://philadel phiabuildings.org/pab/app/ar_display.cfm/23154, and Athenaeum files.

7. Of even greater interest may have been the "portrait" of a medieval architect that formed the frontispiece of Pugin's *The True Principles of Pointed or Christian Architecture* of 1841, with later editions, a book of great influence on nineteenth-century ecclesiastical architecture. The seated figure holds a pair of dividers points down on a drawing.

8. In the Herbert Mitchell Archive, there dated ca. 1890, which seems too late.

9. See Sarah Bradford Landau, *George B. Post, Architect* (New York: Monacelli Press), 1998. There is a group of portraits of shapers of the national AIA in archival storage at the Association's headquarters in Washington. See note 44.

10. David B. Dearinger, ed., *Paintings and Sculpture in the Collection of the National Academy of Design*, vol. 1, 1826–1925 (New York: Hudson Hills Press, 2004), 48. I am not certain which of the paintings

at the AIA and the NAD is the original. There is also a third, inferior version, of the portrait at the AIA headquarters.

11. James F. O'Gorman, ed., *The Makers of Trinity Church in the City of Boston* (Amherst, Mass.: University of Massachusetts Press, 2004), 174; Edward Waldo Forbes, *Saturday Club, a Century Completed, 1920–1956* (Boston, Mass.: Houghton Mifflin, 1958). There is another portrait of Coolidge, dated 1913, by Frank Weston Benson, at Harvard University.

12. Jeffrey T. Schnapp, "The Face of the Modern Architect," *Grey Room* 33 (Fall 2008), 6–25.

13. Otto Friedrich, *Clover* (New York: Simon and Schuster, 1979), 287–91, for example.

14. Mariana Griswold Van Rensselaer's *Henry Hobson Richardson and His Works* Boston, Mass.: Houghton Mifflin, 1888) passim.

15. See James F. O'Gorman, *Living Architecture: A Biography of H.H. Richardson* (New York: Simon & Schuster Editions, 1997), and idem, *Henry Hobson Richardson and His Office: Selected Drawings* (Cambridge, Mass.: Harvard College Library, 1974).

16. "The English Artist, Herkomer," *Northern Christian Advocate*, 7 December 1882, 3.

17. See Lee M. Edwards, "Hubert Herkomer in America," *American Art Journal* 21 (1989), 48–73, esp. 65–69.

18. The Coops and the private study were described and photographed many times. See O'Gorman, *Richardson and His Office*, 4–13.

19. The contents of Richardson's study (of which several vintage photographs survive) were catalogued for probate at his death (including his large library, now at Special Collections, Loeb Library, Harvard University), but art works such as the image of the Colleoni are not listed. Available at the Norfolk County Court House, Dedham, Massachusetts: Registry of Probate 24978. Edwards, "Hubert Herkomer," calls the Colleoni a "small bronze copy," but it is not small and is clearly shown as a photograph in photographs of the room itself. Herkomer's brushwork here makes it look like a sketch. Richardson's collection of photographs, also housed at Special Collections in the Loeb Library, contains many prints from Venice and five images of the Colleoni, one of which conforms to the viewpoint of the photo in the studio but is much smaller (volume 310). For the architect's brief account of his Venetian sojourn see James F. O'Gorman, "On

Vacation with H. H. Richardson: Ten Letters from Europe, 1882," *Archives of American Art Journal* 19 (1979), 2–14.

20. See J. J. Glessner, *The Story of a House* (1923; repr., Chicago: Glessner House Museum, 2011), 13. An intended etching of the portrait never materialized.

21. *Boston Daily Transcript*, 7 July 1886, 4, as reported in the *New Orleans Daily Picayune*, 12 July 1886.

22. See Charles Moore, *Daniel H. Burnham, Architect, Planner of Cities* (Boston: Houghton Mifflin, 1921 (reissued by Da Capo Press, 1968) and Thomas S. Hines, *Burnham of Chicago, Architect and Planner* (New York: Oxford University Press, 1974).

23. William and Willow Hagans, *Zorn in America* (New York: The Swedish-American Historical Society, 2009), 152–54.

24. See Everard M. Upjohn, *Richard Upjohn, Architect and Churchman* (New York: Columbia University Press, 1939). The frontispiece there is a reproduction of another portrait of the architect, unattributed and devoid of any obvious iconographical detail. See also Saylor, *The A.I.A.'s First Hundred Years*, opp. p. 41.

25. Reproduced at the Library of Congress website: http://lcweb2.loc.gov/cgi-bin/query.

26. Although it lies outside the chronological limit of this investigation, it is worth noting a portrait that carries this typology well into the twentieth century: that of Maine's John Calvin Stevens of 1935 by Claude W. Montgomery (1912–90) at the Portland Museum of Art. The eighty-year-old sits in a chair before a fireplace frame. The painting to his left refers to Stevens's alternate career as an artist and his deep involvement in all phases of the history of the Museum. See below in the text.

27. Woods, *From Craft to Profession*, 118.

28. See O'Gorman, *Living Architecture*, 152, for example. When Frederick Law Olmsted and Charles Sprague Sargent sponsored Van Rensselaer's 1888 monograph on the architect, they (or she, or Richardson's successors) chose as frontispiece a formal head-and-shoulders image that presents him looking like any other businessman and robs him of his unique personality. As Carla Yanni has observed, the production of the book was as much business venture as memorial: "'The Richardson Memorial,' Marianna Griswold Van Rensselaer's *Henry Hobson Richardson and His Works*," *Nineteenth Century* 27 (Fall 2007), 27–36.

29. See [Frederick J. Squires, with illustrations by Rockwell Kent], *Architec-tonics: the Tales of Tom Thumtack, Architect* (New York: The William T. Comstock Company, 1914). For a brief description of this little-remarked publication (outside of Kent studies) see James F. O'Gorman, "The Tales of Tom Thumtack, Architect," *Nineteenth Century* 31 (Spring 2011), 24–29.

30. Nor did they seem to want to be seen in public with such accouterments. For example, a letter of 15 April 1901 from Burnham to Frederick Law Olmsted, Jr., when the two were part of the team designing what has been called the MacMillan Plan for Washington, DC, makes clear that on supervising trips to the site a draftsman would accompany them, perhaps so that they might look unencumbered and managerial. Burnham in this instance, however, doubts "the advisability of taking a draftsman with us." Burnham Letters (CA1), Ryerson and Burnham Library, Art Institute of Chicago.

31. Saylor, *The A.I.A.'s First Hundred Years*, 36.

32. James F. O'Gorman and Earle G. Shettleworth, Jr., *The Maine Perspective: Architectural Drawings, 1800–1980* (Portland, Maine: The Portland Museum of Art, 2006), 68. There exists a drawing of Daniel Burnham in the drafting room of the Chicago World's Fair of 1893 by the illustrator Thure de Thulstrup that also reflects this division. A standing Burnham leans comfortably against a drafting table, hands empty, while a seated Charles B. Atwood, hardly a no-name architect, plies his pencil, as do other draftsmen in the background. Moore, *Burnham*, 48.

33. There are plenty of exceptions, of course, especially after the beginning of the twentieth century when the profession was assured. And one must consider the various personalities involved. There is, for example, an informal photograph of Henry Hornbostel (1867–1961), probably from the 1920s, taken at Carnegie Tech with some of his draftsmen. All are in shirtsleeves and devoid of instruments, but pipes and cigars, including Hornbostel's, are in evidence. Kidney, *Hornbostel*, 194.

34. Margaret Heilbrun., ed., *Inventing the Skyline: The Architecture of Cass Gilber* (New York: Columbia University Press, 2000,) 6, 21; Smithsonian Art Inventories Catalog.

35. As a comparison it should be noted that, of the fifteen portraits of architects who served as presidents of RIBA, 1835–1899, reproduced in J. A. Gotch, ed., *The Growth and Work of the Royal Institute of*

British Architects (London: The R.I.B.A., 1934), ten hold nothing, two hold books, and three are shown with drawings. The British architect aspired to comparison to the aristocratic rather than the managerial class, as did American architects, but the principle is the same.

36. Richard Oliver, *Bertram Grosvenor Goodhue* (Cambridge, Mass.: MIT Press, 1983). For Day, see Patricia J. Fanning, *Through an Uncommon Lens: The Life and Photography of F. Holland Day* (Amherst, MA: University of Massachusetts Press, 2008).

37. Walter C. Kidney, *Henry Hornbostel* (Pittsburgh, PA: Roberts Rinehardt, 2002), opp. 1.

38. Earle G. Shettleworth, Jr., "John Calvin Stevens's Architectural Library," in *American Architects and Their Books, 1940–1915*, eds. Kenneth Hefertepe and James F. O'Gorman (Amherst, Mass.: University of Massachusetts Press, 2007), 215–230 and frontispiece.

39. Hines, *Burnham*, 70.

40. See Jhennefer A. Amundson, ed., *Thomas U. Walter: The Lectures on Architecture, 1841–53*, Philadelphia, PA: The Athenaeum, 2006). A series of later photographic portraits of Walter shows the aging architect in similar format.

41. See Davis McNeely Stauffer, "Lithographic Portraits of Albert Newsam," *Pennsylvania Magazine* 24 (1900), 446. Walter's account book at the Athenaeum of Philadelphia records Neagle's receipt for payment for the oil portrait: $180.00 on July 7, 1835. The bottom of the original canvas was trimmed to match the dimensions of a later portrait of Walter's wife (also by Neagle and also at the Athenaeum) loosing the crucial details of scale and book recorded by Newsam. On the other hand, the lithographer omitted the view of Moyamensing Prison found on the canvas.

42. Woods, *From Craft to Profession*, 169.

43. Most of these are illustrated in Wilbert R. Hasbrouck, *The Chicago Architectural Club* (New York: Monacelli Press, 2005), 436–38. Further information from the files of the Chicago History Museum.

44. Although the paintings were offered to the Historical Society in 1943 for the purpose of placing them on "suitable display" in a "permanent exhibit," these portraits now rest in the bowels of the Museum and may be seen by appointment only.

45. Hood Museum files; Kathleen A. Foster, *Thomas Eakins Rediscovered* (New Haven, CT: Yale University Press, 1997).

46. See "Notable Gift to the Germania Club," *Fine Arts Journal* 32 (March 1915), n. p.

47. *Fine Arts Journal* 37 (March 1919), 2–3; *Chicago Daily Tribune*, 16 February 1919, D2: "The pose . . . is decidedly poor . . . . The modeling of the figure is weak. The flesh is soft. . . . The feeling of the bone quality of the hand is equally soft . . . . The quality of the material of the suit is decidedly poor. The face is not a particularly strong one," etc. One wonders what painting she was looking at. *Chicago Daily Tribune*, 17 January 1926, B3.

48. Information from the files of the Chicago History Museum.

49. Richard Ormond and Elaine Kilmurray, *John Singer Sargent: Portraits of the 1890s* (New Haven, CT: Yale University Press, 2002), 99–101 (Cat. 319); Baker, *Hunt*, 428–31. Hunt began posing in May and died in July. His wife disliked the painting because, she wrote, "it represents a man thin and worn from suffering," and many others who knew him also gave the work mixed reviews. At this distant time the pathos is gone and the heroic image remains.

50. Olmsted's is equal in size to Hunt's but shows a much humbler figure. Portraits of American architects in the buildings they designed (as opposed to their names alone) are relatively rare but not unknown, especially in the late nineteenth century and early twentieth. Hunt's profile by Karl Bitter appears in his Marble House in Newport, Rhode Island, for William K. Vanderbilt. Some are caricatures, as is that of Cass Gilbert in the lobby of his Woolworth Building in New York.

51. Woods, *From Craft to Profession*, 104.

52. Inscriptions or plaques in public places dedicated to architects do exist. None of them come near rivaling Hunt's monument on Fifth Avenue, but it might be noted that a full-length sculpted figure by Lee Lawrie of Bertram Grosvenor Goodhue (1869–1924) lies in medieval fashion on his tomb at the Church of the Intercession in New York. Romy Wyllie, *Bertram Goodhue: His Life and Residential Architecture* (New York: W.W. Norton & Company, 2007), 193.

53. What might be a caricatured allusion to such full-length figures appears in the portrait of the "architect" in [Squires], *Architec-tonics*. The caricature is another way of picturing the architect that deserves consideration. See, for example, Theodore L. Wust's of Daniel Burnham as Director of the Works at the Chicago Fair of 1893, in which the dwarfish architect stands on an unrolled sheet of drawings holding a yard stick while steelwork rises in the background. Hines, *Burnham*

of Chicago, 93; the work is now in the collection of the Chicago History Museum. Another, of St. Louis architect Harry G. Clymer (1873–1958), shows him holding dividers points down on a drawing. See "Cartoonists and Caricaturists of the Daily Press," in *St. Louisians As We See 'Em* (St. Louis: A Noble Printing Company, 1903?).

Epilogue

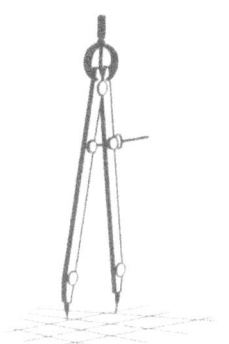

This brief study has surveyed the way some architects, through the media of their portraitists, projected a changing image of themselves over the course of the nineteenth century. Many of the later men did sit at drafting tables, and, as we have seen, did occasionally have themselves represented at work, although more often in informal photographs rather than publicity pictures. The history of the evolving profession accounts for the varying ways in which architectural portraiture was realized, just as portraiture reflects that history. When we compare the image of Neagle's *John Haviland*, say, with that of Sargent's *Richard Morris Hunt*, we have a quick and dramatic pictorial summation of the evolution of the profession over its first century. The quest for represented stature we find in Peale's *Buckland* had come to full flower by the time of Hunt's demise.

Index

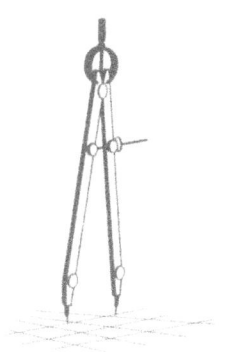